The
Broken
SCOUT

A Story of Abuse and Redemption

The Broken SCOUT

A Story of Abuse and Redemption

Thomas Gregory Stewart

REDEMPTION
PRESS

Published by Redemption Press, PO Box 427, Enumclaw, WA 98022

Toll Free (844) 2REDEEM (273-3336)

Redemption Press is honored to present this title in partnership with the author. The views expressed or implied in this work are those of the author. Redemption Press provides our imprint seal representing design excellence, creative content, and high quality production.

The events in this memoir are portrayed to the best of Tom Stewart's memory. While all the stories in this book are true, some names and identifying details have been changed to protect the privacy of the people involved.

All Scripture quotations, unless otherwise indicated, are taken from the *Holy Bible, New International Version®. NIV®.* Copyright © 1973, 1978, 1984 by International Bible Society. Used by permission of Zondervan. All rights reserved.

ISBN 13: 978-1-68314-011-5 (Print)

978-1-68314-012-2 (Hard Cover)

978-1-68314-013-9 (ePub)

978-1-68314-014-6 (Mobi)

Library of Congress Catalog Card Number: 2016960858

You intended to harm me, but God intended it for good to accomplish what is now being done, the saving of many lives.
—Genesis 50:20

DEDICATION

THIS BOOK IS dedicated to my late son, Benjamin Thomas Stewart. His death was the catalyst for understanding God's ultimate purpose for me. I love you Benny! Fly my son, soar high.

CONTENTS

ONE

THE SECRET

FEELING LIKE MY little Tommy self who just might get into big trouble, I stand still in the hallway leading to the kitchen. My heart beats fast as a sense of panic erodes my determination.

I hear her in there. My mother. I hear her filling up the teakettle to make her breakfast tea. A worn wooden chair scrapes as she pulls it in to the table. The morning edition of the *News Tribune* rustles as she waits for the kettle to boil.

Maybe she's hoping today's local section will include one of her two sons' many achievements. She clips and gloats over any article that highlights the Stewart name; especially the sports highlights, then pastes them into what she called her many "*Snips and Snaps*" scrapbooks, as if they're proof that no one's children are better than hers.

That's me all right. Thomas Gregory Stewart. *Her oldest trophy.* I've been customized, shaped, and molded into the perfect son, perfect scholar, perfect church kid, perfect athlete, perfect musician. And, oh yes, the perfect Boy Scout. Diligent and disciplined, just like Mom—Betty Lou—orders me to be.

Perfectly shamed and miserable.

Nothing was ever allowed to interfere with Mom's pursuit of admiration and envy of others. Especially my feelings. Her all-consuming

Stewart pride parallels materialism . . . and the price tag is dangling over my head.

I hesitate in the hallway, on the verge of pivoting 180 degrees around and tiptoeing back to my room. I'd do anything . . . anything . . . to avoid the conversation ahead. *Should I even risk it?* She's probably not going to believe me anyway.

I may be eighteen, but I feel like the shy little boy I was ten years ago when all the bad stuff started. My nightmare. This is not going to be an "acceptable" discussion no matter what I say. *Why am I so afraid to talk to her?* This talk should have taken place way back then. But it didn't. If it had, would it have prevented what happened to me? Would it have saved my stolen childhood? I have avoided the inevitable, as long as possible, but can no longer hide behind the "perfection" I've tried to achieve for her sake.

I've been trying to cry out for help, but she hasn't heard my silent screams. So, I just got used to it and stood at attention for her next instruction; never really feeling like a son, but more like a symbol of her pride.

Depending on the little bit of courage I have, the weight of my shattered dreams is what is holding me back. What *he* did to me. Deceived me and coaxed me until my young mind was drawn into quicksand. He was a thief who brainwashed me and stole my understanding of who I was, and changed me into who I am.

So did she.

The kettle's sudden piercing whistle startles me. I stop at the doorway; my heart pounding, waiting for her to notice me so I don't have to make the first move. Just in case my courage caves in, I don't make a sound.

The adrenaline pouring through my body is making it hard for me to focus.

Mom still doesn't look up at me. She must not realize I am standing here. She's so engrossed in her paper, I could still back up without her even noticing.

I know what I am going to tell her will taint her perfect vision of me. Will it irrevocably diminish her self-centered impression of me; her overachieving, prized-possession son? That is the only bond—the only connection I have ever known between us . . . as long as I kept my opinions to myself.

Hey, I'm a grown man now. Why am I so reluctant? Obviously, for the same reason I have been so scared to say anything for the past ten years. Mom's had a plan for me all along. All my reactions, desires, and passions have been engineered by that plan.

I haven't been honest with her. She doesn't deal well with dishonesty.

With her, there's no mercy and no grace for anything that hasn't been designated by her.

I've dreaded this moment for a long time, but knew it had to come. With my feet firmly planted, I stand up straighter, and reach up to grab ahold and hang on to the molding above the doorway. She acknowledges my presence by glancing back at me over her right shoulder, then does a double take when she sees the serious look on my face.

With that one look, my body feels as if it is going to collapse.

I've grown up with her stare that looks right through me, but today it's getting to me as never before. Her eyes squint as if zooming in, while her eyebrows plunge sternly. My empty stomach growls, feeling as if it is being yanked inside out and exposed.

With a surge of adrenaline, I manage to mumble, ". . . Um . . ."

Annoyed, she gruffly clears her throat and swings her head back to tell me, "We Stewarts do not ever use the word 'um.'"

"Yes . . . Mother . . . sorry," I gulp.

Her mood doesn't look promising. My voice is choked by the density exuding from her. My determination quickly reverts back to my usual passive response to her customary mind control. I've never been allowed to join in any conversation. They are always lectures, where my participation is to only listen and agree—and that's it. Straightening up to all 6'3" of me, I drop my hold to clasp my palms together, fingers tightly intertwined, and finally speak. "Mom, I have something to tell you. Something really important."

I want to scream at her to stop fiddling with her teacup. She's always hammered respect for all authority figures, especially her and Dad, into me. No questions . . . no back talk allowed . . . ever.

I fumble out, "Mom, do you know what Bruce did to me?" I wait for a second. "Bruce hurt me. He really hurt me. He hurt me for over ten years."

Her face registers surprise at first. Then she closes her eyes in either denial or anger; *I can't tell.* She shifts back around in her chair facing the table in absolute silence. Mom is rarely silent in a confrontation. It's the rest of us who usually are. If she doesn't get her way, there is no positive outcome for anyone. She crosses her arms in front of her, as if in a childish temper tantrum. I wait for what comes next. Mom is unpredictable. Her unstable moods can swing anywhere from plunging deep down into a black hole up to catapulting into the unknown. Her responses are usually full of out-of-proportion rage. As her son, I've witnessed signs of what could be a progressive mental disorder. It would have to be. Others have also hinted there must be something wrong with my mom.

Her blank reaction accelerates my frustration. "Mom, do you realize what I am saying?"

She continues to ignore me, looks down and scowls, as if the answer is in her teacup. No reaction. No response.

"Mom, did you hear me?" *I've never spoken to her like this before.* "Mom, Bruce molested me. He abused me!"

She exhales a sharp sigh of disgust. Her back straightens to meet the high back of the spindled wooden chair. A look of repulsion crosses her face.

Is she trying to process what Bruce did to me . . . her little boy?
I think she is. Oh, I'm so relieved.
She believes me! What was I so afraid of? Why did I wait so long?

Maybe what I endured will be a wake-up call to her. Maybe it will humble her, spark some good in her. Maybe my sacrifice was not in vain. My mother finally looks up at me. Murmuring under her breath, she slides the position of her chair backwards until it hits the wall.

Crumpling the newspaper towards the center of the table, almost spilling what is left of her tea, she bolts up out of her chair and stomps hard toward me with her eyes laser-focused at mine. In a screech that rises in volume and echoes down the hall, she yells in my face, "How dare you even talk about your scoutmaster like that?"

I feel as if I'm going to throw up. The pain of my mother's words feels worse than if she had kicked me in the gut. Then I know. *She doesn't believe me.* My mother's not going to stand by me. *I'm not surprised.*

I try to contain my body's shaking as the tension in the room builds. "Mother, why do you think Bruce was so interested in helping me all the time? All those Boy Scout badges and patches? I earned them only when he got what he wanted from me."

She glares and accuses me, "You're lying, Tom! Bruce would never do such a thing!"

Desperate, I say, "I am not lying Mom. I wouldn't lie to you. He threatened me with a gun; pointing it at my head. He said he would kill my family if I didn't do what he said. He said he would kill you, Mom."

She's shaking, she's so mad. There's no way she's backing down. In the silence, I feel myself regressing and lower my eyes to the floor. *I had no voice then, I have no voice now.* There is nothing left to say except, "Mom, I'm sorry you feel that way."

Without lifting my face, I turn away, and head back to my room, devastated. *My own mother is not going to accept what I said. I lose again; she wins again.*

I am that little boy again—Tommy—who packed up his soul so long ago, the boy who concealed his pain in a safe no one had the combination to open. Having been stuck so long, the pain absorbed into who I am. What happened to me was like a perpetual sleepwalking dream I was unable to wake from.

Repeatedly, I had hoped my mom would come to invade the dream and wake me, rescue me, and comfort me. But my need to matter had been ignored. Even now, I continue to be stifled. *Why didn't anyone see what was going on? Didn't I matter? I still don't matter.*

Maybe Mom is right? *How dare I insult Bruce this way?* I feel as if I should apologize for even bringing it up.

Confused, I tipped toward the beginnings of what felt like anger toward my mother. Anger is not a place where I let myself go.

My walk back down the hall to my room feels like one of those movie scenes where it keeps going and going with no end—stuck, unable to go anywhere. I'm surrounded by Mother's gallery of portraits hanging on both sides of me. *Oh, yes,* the Stewart family—posed in our tacky matching outfits, with on-cue smiles on our faces. It wasn't often I smiled without being told to.

I see reality now. It's all been a facade. I am awakening from my mother's mind control, and I see how dysfunctional us Stewarts really are.

I won't look back. I don't want her to see the final blow of defeat she left on my face. I have tried to be the best son possible to her. No disrespect, no disobedience. I never said anything except, "Yes, Mother."

Facing forward, I raise my head up high and pull myself together, shutting out her denial behind my bedroom door.

TWO

THE HAPPY BEFORE

CRASHING ON MY bed, I was determined not to think about what just happened. I was good at blocking out hurts. I just shut them off like it was normal and pretended I was fine. I had to get through the rest of this day so I could arrive at tomorrow; onward to my destination out of here . . . college.

Get over it, Tom. It is what it is. Just as I expected.

Still, no child should ever have to experience what I did. Never did I think that the Stewart pride could sink that low. *I'm her son.* At least my timing was perfect for once. I will only have to tolerate her for a short while until I leave this place. Otherwise, I don't know how long I could have kept my cool. What kind of mother would not believe their own child? That would be my kind of mother! The one whose pride is more important than me.

The courage I somehow found to tell her pushed me into finally doing it. Foolish to think that there was no one better to tell than my own mother. Assuming, *Oh, she will listen—I know she will.*

I had envisioned her marching straight down to the police station before Bruce even had a chance to fabricate his excuses. She'd be the one person who'd never let anyone get by with endangering her son. Bruce's brainwashing couldn't compete with the wrath of Betty Lou.

Footsteps outside my room interrupted my thoughts. Dreading another encounter with Mom, I was relieved when I recognized Dad's firm knock on my door.

What's he doing home? Did he stay home from work today? I wasn't used to him being home. I hope he didn't overhear Mother and me.

Like clockwork, his daily grind began before the sun came up for his all-consuming career. Dad's job as the personnel manager at American Plywood Association was his life. It defined him and stroked his ego. When introducing himself, he would take a deep breath, puff out his chest, and make sure they knew he was the top dog in the wood products industry.

As he entered my room, his eyes probed mine and asked me, "Do you have a minute?"

"Sure, Dad. Everything okay?"

My nerves were impatiently waiting for him to confront me about Mom.

I moved over on the bed to make room for him to sit down and asked, "Where's Mom?"

"She went to lie down." I didn't know what to say.

Dad's face looked tired, but it looked like he wanted to tell me something. Sit-down conversations between us didn't happen that often. When we did talk, it was usually to casually catch up or simply shoot the breeze. So, this really caught me off guard, and not like him at all.

As he starts in, "I remember when I was your age, Tom, graduating and heading off to college," I release my worry, *Oh, good, it's not about what I told Mom.* Even if it was about what I told her, I doubted Dad could ever make me feel as worthless as she did.

He chuckled softly and muttered something about wanting to give me some "valuable fatherly advice" before leaving the nest. It was the same chuckle that often preceded his launching into a familiar story. I tried to relax, preparing myself to listen and humor him. There was something different in his manner this time and I leaned forward.

Dad grinned in his easygoing way and rested his hand briefly on my shoulder. He was starting in on how great things were "way back when"—what I interpreted as *the happy before.*

I thought about how I'd never experienced too many days when I was anywhere close to being happy, but tried to enter into the mood he was in.

"Remember what happened the night before my graduation?" He shot me a quick glance to see if I was with him. "When everything went wrong for me? When my dream of walking with my graduating class wearing my burgundy cap and gown with the gold honor tassels ruptured just as my appendix did?"

I could have probably told Dad's story verbatim from memory. But I liked hearing him tell it. Maybe this time Dad will reveal the parts he has kept to himself. There had to be something more to this Stewart saga I was born in to. "So . . . with the only ambulance in town called to another emergency, the medics needed to find an alternative mode of transportation to the hospital. They called the most unlikely, but feasible option they could think of—the local funeral home."

He laughed and I manage to laugh in sync with him. "Yes, a hearse. I thought they were joking. They weren't."

"There I was on a stretcher, 'Stay flat,' they told me. I couldn't do much else besides freak out. The medic tried a little morbid humor. 'Well, young man, if your appendix ruptures, and we can't get you to the hospital in time, your body will be all ready for the coroner. I am kidding of course.' By then my pain was getting excruciating. That's when I passed out."

Still enjoying his recounting, Dad picked it up as he was waking up in the recovery room.

"All I remember is opening my eyes to a nurse with stunning eyes leaning over me saying, 'Hello, Robert, I am your nurse, Betty Lou, and I will be taking care of you.' I focused my eyes on her mouth and the bright red lipstick outlining her heart-shaped lips."

"'You are truly something, Miss Betty Lou. May I call you Betty Lou?' Babbling from the medication, I tried to make my voice as manly as I could. 'And by the way, Miss Betty Lou, how old are you?'"

"Her flirtatious grin turned into a beautiful white smile. 'Well,' she said, 'According to your chart, Mr. Stewart, I am an older woman; but only by a year and three days.'"

Dad was now well into his story, enjoying himself reliving the familiar details. "She was a nurse in training, and her instructor was an older lady named Bertha."

I sighed under my breath, knowing what always came next through his judgmental Stewart mouth. "Bertha was very hefty." He laughs. "I kept dozing in and out, but managed to fight the urge to sleep; I didn't want to lose any time with my new love at first sight."

"I told Betty Lou, 'Thank you for taking care of me. May I tip you?'

Betty Lou blushed while she was writing on her clipboard, and flirted back, 'I'm flattered.' She had a calming peace about her. The way she moved around my bed helped me drift my way back to sleep, falling into a dream of my mother coming to me and leaning over my bed in the same way. But, I knew it was only a dream. Mom was committed to Western State Mental Hospital when I was only thirteen."

"I woke hearing a mechanical beep, and lay there in my hospital bed trying to keep myself alert. Tom, I thought how strange it was that your mom was the first lady who had comforted my soul in a place that had been empty since Grandma had to leave."

Dad paused. "I've heard somewhere that men sometimes seek out women who are like their own mothers. Please listen carefully, Son . . . be very, very cautious with your choices. You know what I am saying, right?"

This part of his usual rerun of his love story was different than usual. *He must be warning me to never marry someone like Mom.*

Mom and Dad were married on April 4, 1953. In all the pictures from their wedding, they looked so happy; yet, I wondered if those smiles just mimicked the family portraits down the hall.

Typically, after the wedding part of the story, he'd sigh, look away, and his voice would trail off, but he kept going this time. His expression grew serious and his tone lowered to slow and easy.

"Unfortunately, Tom, soon after your mom and I got married, she made the decision to resign from her promising nursing career. Even as the man of the house, I had no say."

No different from today. *I have a feeling where this conversation is going.* Dad seemed more open than ever before. The look of confusion and deep-seated pain on his face was the same as the one he wore when he originally told me of his own mother's mental illness.

I always wondered why my parents acted the way they did. Why were their emotions so conflicted? I knew there had to be far more, or maybe far less, to their relationship than he ever let on. Being their son, I could see a disconnect in their souls; drifting far away from each other. It just so happens that Mother lost her mom when she was thirteen; the same age Dad was when he had to live without his. Understandably, with both of my parents growing up as only children, then considering how they both lost their mothers at a very important age, it surely explains a lot. I could hear from the huskiness in his voice that he was trying to contain himself as best he could.

"You know, Tom, those once-happy days were short-lived, and soon became pure frustration for me. After we were married, not only did she quit her job, she hired a housekeeper, and a gardener, and even bribed the milkman to come in the house and bake for her. What was supposed to be a happily ever after, became me living in a world according to Betty Lou." I had heard enough, and didn't want to hear about Mom anymore. I was stuck somewhere between the few happy times of the past that were so sacred to Dad, and the reality of Mom's true dark colors that we lived with now. It sounded to me like Dad was more of a father to Mother than her husband. A cold feeling went through me as I thought about what he had gone through for the past twenty-seven years.

"How did you do it, Dad? How did you actually keep going?"

Dad smiled. "Well, Son, having children helped. You were a long-awaited and welcome change."

I admired Dad for sticking by Mom. No matter how many times she hurt him, he never talked about her with disrespect.

Grandpa Cecil demonstrated that same Stewart loyalty with Grandma Alice even after she went to the mental hospital at Western State. There, she was diagnosed with schizophrenia. When he visited her, she'd get so worked up, they insisted he stop coming. Grandpa was devastated. The marriage ended and he remarried in an attempt to fill his hurt.

Trying to lighten the mood, Dad shifted forward to their making babies story. I squirmed, not wanting to hear this part. He reminded me of the hard time they had conceiving. In fact, they kept trying for over nine years without any luck.

"There were times that she called me at work in the middle of the afternoon, she didn't care if she was interrupting a meeting or not, and demanded I come home immediately. 'It's time, you have to come home right now.'"

I winced; not being comfortable thinking of my parents in that way. "Finally; as you know, on October 6, 1962, nine years, six months and two days after Betty Lou Hansen became Mrs. Robert Cecil Stewart, you arrived, Tom." Dad stopped talking, looked down at his hands, and solemnly said, "Something drastically changed in your mom then. It was troubling. Being a new mother must have weighed so heavily on her."

We sat in silence. I didn't want Dad to stop talking—he had never been this open before about anything.

"So, Dad," I asked. "Did things ever get any better?"

He shrugged his shoulders and shook his head. "By the time that she finally had you, she was already thirty-four, and then thirty-six when she had your brother. I don't know if things got worse, or just more peculiar."

I wanted to commend him on his loyalty and tolerance as a husband in their marriage but Dad wasn't through yet. "With your brother, Matt, also being an October baby, she had her mind set on what she thought would be unique. She wanted to name him Huckley! Believe it or not!" He snorted. "We were going to have our own little Tom and Huck."

"That was one time in our marriage I put my foot down! I insisted on anything but a name like that. I didn't back down, and we actually agreed on the name of Matthew. I believe that was the only thing she ever conceded to me." I thought, *I'm sure Matt appreciates that.*

"You never told me that part of the story before."

Mom may not have gotten her way with the "Adventures of Tom and Huck," but the continuing saga of the Stewarts has been far more intriguing. Dad frowned, the same familiar complicit frown, a "goes-without-saying" look that we often shared, depending on Mom's mood. The look signified an unspoken *"uh-oh"* between us, and nothing else needed to be said.

Finally, Dad was done. He seemed at peace, as if he had come to terms with feelings he had padlocked at his core for too long. Maybe he had accepted not receiving in return the same respect he gave his wife. And, that was surely something that we could relate to and talk about.

For the first time, I separated my history with Mom long enough to consider Dad's solitary position as her husband. That explains why he is so attached to his work. I; too, did anything I could to avoid being at home. Things like deliberately taking the hour-long bus ride home from school—twice. I looked at Dad with new eyes, feeling sorry for what he had gone through; the same sorry I felt for myself. I knew I resented Mom, and needed to let go of that. Being weighed down for so long by her overbearing attitude put me in the same place emotionally where Dad was. We were both exhausted from never living up to her expectations. Once I took the focus away from how sorry I felt for myself, I could understand why Dad had been so absent from the family. I felt ashamed for being so judgmental. God has such a way of humbling us that can't be denied.

Dad stood up, looking lighter than when he walked in. He extended his hand to shake mine—his equivalent of a hug. "I am proud of you, Son. You have done an excellent job."

Dad's approval meant everything to me. As the door closed behind him, my jaw dropped. I was ashamed of myself. Until then, I had resented his passivity for so long. It kept me from opening my eyes to the real reason he was hiding behind.

THREE

FULL CLOSETS

THIS DAY SURE had turned out just as unpredictable as the gloomy weather outside. *Well, no better time to tackle my packing if I'm going to get out of here.*

I tapped on the touch-lamp on my desk next to the same bed I've slept on since I was a boy. In the same cluttered room. The house had been overflowing from my mom's hoarding since the day they moved in right after I was born. My room has been sort of a shared storage locker. It was a safety hazard just moving around. Bundles of old newspapers from the past eighteen years had accumulated in every available spot of what was supposed to be my bedroom. A very limited few were ever allowed in our home or were aware of the conditions inside our prison. No visitors were allowed in the cell blocks of our bedrooms. Probably a good thing. It was embarrassing. Matt's time warp of a room still had the baby-themed wallpaper on his walls. A baby scale with a giraffe motif was still sitting on his dresser.

We didn't have any say about our rooms. Nothing was worth causing a reaction from Mom.

My socks and underwear were jammed in the one remaining top drawer she left for me. What little bit of clothing I had hung on a child-sized clothing rack from my own nursery. My small desk, squeezed into that little corner, was the only spot that reflected part of me. Perfectly arranged, not for my mom's sake, but mine. In the middle of my rigorous schedule of performance for Mom, I desperately tried to protect my immediate bubble of space, occasionally succeeding. I figured I had Mom to thank for my precise habits of tidiness—a reaction to all this clutter, I suppose.

Time to look for my suitcase. It wasn't in my bedroom, so the scavenger hunt began. I didn't know which cupboard or closet I should risk opening. The hall closet was overflowing with purses—so many that the sliding closet door bulged out from the pressure.

Mom was a collector—if that's what you want to call it. Her shoes overflowed from her closet to underneath her bed. There were not enough days in the year to wear each pair. Outdated pairs were packed away in the basement, next to the out-of-style outfits that used to complement the shoes. Nothing was ever given away or donated—"They might be back in style someday" is what Mother said.

Dad's job was a good one, but how could his salary provide for all she had accumulated in this stockpile of a house? I'd never accuse her of stealing anything I hadn't witnessed already, but she seemed to feel entitled to have everything she wanted that would fit into her purse.

Dad wasn't truly innocent either. He was the one who taught us to sneak whatever food we could fit into our pockets at his favorite all-you-can-eat buffet. His participation cheered on Mom's habit of snatching up salt-and-pepper shakers, napkin holders, and silverware from restaurants. At home, towels and washcloths would show up out of nowhere with hotel names imprinted on them. Just like the silver holiday platter in the China hutch that had Olympic Hotel engraved on it. I was sure thankful that this kleptomaniac trait didn't seem to be hereditary with me.

Was my suitcase in the entry coat closet? "Open at your own risk," I muttered, low enough so Mom couldn't overhear. I didn't hear her; *she must still be in her room.* As I eased the door open, I stepped back cautiously to avoid any falling hazards. I turned the handle to the right but it didn't budge. Reversing the turn to the left, I heard a click and felt a heavy tension that warned me not to open it any further. I reached my left arm around inside the crack of the door to stabilize whatever was teetering. Now, with the door fully open, I supported the ceiling-high stack of boxes with my upper body.

After all of that, the suitcase was still nowhere to be found. I couldn't figure out why she kept this stuff. Saving our cut fingernail trimmings in a jar surely isn't normal. It's understandable to hold on to our first haircut clippings, but every haircut to this day? Maybe she was trying to replace feelings of abandonment after the loss of her mother? It was an unsolved mystery isolated behind years of unreachable hurt she didn't know how to express; sometimes rumbling like a freight train through her words and actions.

I'm guessing my own closet is where I should have looked in the first place. I knew there was a reason I didn't. This was a space I avoided. Sliding the left side of the closet open, I forgot how jam-packed full it was of the reminders of my now-exposed secret—Boy Scout awards, plaques, and various up-sized uniforms outfitted with many merit badges. Hanging there was the proof of my commitment, endurance, and just plain hard work, on behalf of the Stewart name. I could swear I heard Bruce's voice shouting my name, as if played in stereo, blaring in my head—"Tom! Tom!" A rush of adrenaline filled my body as I recalled his threats. "If you ever tell anyone, I'll . . ." Then a flashback of the gun he kept tucked away in the back of his pants made me just want to slide the door closed again.

But no, I can't do that. I can't pretend it didn't happen—like Mother just did. I know now that my worth was valued only by what I did—and that was all stored in front of me. As for who I am, it was all summed up by a slap in the face from her Stewart pride.

I found the suitcase on the top shelf, but it had just as much pain attached to it as everything else. All I wanted to do was push the reality of what happened to the back of the closet with my other triggers. It was much easier to just bury it all and pretend it never happened. As I always did. I wasn't sure what hurt more. The abuse from Bruce, or the abuse from my mother. Both happened behind closed doors; both were secrets. Both were completely different, but just as painful.

It's crazy, but there were times I actually preferred being with Bruce than being around my mother. *Was that sick?* Bruce may have violated my body, but my mother violated everything else about me.

If Mom didn't believe me, how could anyone else? She had to be living in denial about herself. Who would ever believe me about my mom's abuse? She was too good of an actress. But it was abuse all right. Different than what Bruce did to me, but abuse still the same. All my warped memories were fused together as one. I couldn't shut them out.

What mother of a teenage boy would pick the lock on the bathroom door while he was in there? My privacy didn't stand a chance against her ambushes. She'd crash my private time on the toilet with my pants on the floor.

"You know the drill," she'd demand sternly.

Why in the world—whether she was a nurse or not—was she so adamant about making sure my fifteen-year-old behind was wiped well enough? Somehow, she found joy in poking in violation if the job was not to her specifications. It was gross invasion, her index finger in place of a rectal thermometer. Mortified was not a strong enough word. Oddly, my parents camouflaged their own questionable hygiene with Minipoo Dry Shampoo Powder and Brylcream—their alternative to their maybe once-a-week showers. For Dad, it was a generational thing. For her it was to prevent dirtying another towel, which meant less laundry. Not that she ever did laundry anyway.

We knew not to upset Mom by getting all the stacked boxes in the shower soaking wet. Moving them each time I wanted a shower was not an option.

Mom attempted to convince me her shampoo powder was more convenient, but I preferred to use the showers at school instead. The only other option was running my head under the faucet, obviously not very comfortable at my height.

Still, that was a much better option than my dad had. Mother required him to go to the state park down the street to shower when he got around to wanting one. He got well acquainted with that bathroom. He had claimed it as his master bath since he and his bowels were denied access to the toilet in his own bathroom by the woman of the house. Their relationship was more complex than any equation I had ever computed in high school.

Fumbling through my desk drawer, I gathered up some pens, pads, and some other supplies that could come in handy in school. While rifling through, I came across what I referred to as "The torment book." In other words, the famous Dr. Spock book. The book Mother depended on to raise me right.

Leaning back in my desk chair, I started to recall why Mother thought this book of advice was so helpful. She believed her instincts were in cahoots with Dr. Spock. He was her idol and confidant in child rearing perfection, but she went a little too far when she still referred to it as of late. There was a reason I hid it.

On one of her meddling night patrols, after I thought she'd gone to bed, she caught me. *Why can't she just leave me alone?* "We Stewarts never participate in any vile acts of crudeness," she hissed. "Masturbation is a sin, Thomas Gregory Stewart! God's wrath will come upon you if you continue." Her hell and damnation reference echoed through the house. She'd hold up Dr. Spock's book and shake it as her reinforcement. I had no idea what I was doing was bad. The boys at school always joked about it like it was the cool thing to do.

The subject of sex, and anything associated with it, was taboo to Mother. Forbidden. Sex education in ninth grade bionomics class was just one more opportunity for her to add to my geek label at school. Betty Lou's little Tommy was the only student in the entire ninth grade who was not going to be exposed to that sort of dirty teaching. But Mother didn't know Bruce had given me more of an education about sex than probably anyone else in my entire class.

I wasn't too mortified by her control issues, as she had already conditioned me to expect the worst-case scenario from her at any given moment. Whatever she could get her hands on or dig her nose into to keep her perfect boy squeaky clean, she'd do—even though she had no clue what was going on behind the scenes with Bruce.

My memories with the way she disciplined caused a rising resentment. I could still taste the horrible Fels-Naptha soap residue left on my tongue after she washed my mouth out. The heavy-duty laundry soap in its bright yellow bar was advertised as "ideal for pre-treating stains."

"No Stewart will ever use inappropriate language or disrespect me." Betty Lou's lurking presence was around every corner, anticipating broken ground rules. When she did catch Matt or me in the act of saying something she deemed inappropriate, she found satisfaction in doling out punishment. *I was the good kid.* I don't even know what I said to make her get so mad. *It must have been Matt.*

Her pointing finger directed me to the correction zone where I was to go if I got out of line. Left side of the sink, with my feet lined up with the baseboard on the tattered half circle rug. She'd open the right-hand cupboard door, and grab the bar and rub it back and forth on my teeth. It was even worse when I eventually got braces. I'd have to brush them extra hard afterwards to get all the bitter-tasting soap out.

Since I had such a close relationship with the heavy-duty Fels Naptha Laundry Bar Soap, I wrote an informative essay on it in my eleventh-grade chemistry class. I got an A. I wrote the hazards associated with exposure to the ingredients. How it's strictly for laundry—as it's an excellent stain and grease remover. Just so happens that the punishment tool I was forced to ingest contained benzene or naphtha, a toxic, cancer-causing chemical. Used in excess, it was proven to cause leukemia, kidney cancer, and neurological damage. *I wonder if I really wrote the essay to expose what Mother was doing behind our closed doors? I don't know for sure.* When I showed her the paper, she didn't respond to me. *Did I see a hint of regret in her eyes? I doubt it.* Denial was her best trait.

Since the facts on my essay didn't register with Mom on how dangerous the soap was, I took it upon myself to throw out the three bars stashed in the laundry room cupboard, along with the remaining chunk under the kitchen sink—never to be tasted again.

FOUR

THE BULLY

AS I WAS finishing up my packing for college, I wondered if I should go and talk to Mom and make things right between us. *Should I apologize?* I wanted to leave on good terms for my own sake. Never having stood up to Mother before, I couldn't tell if I felt guilty or not. But quickly changed my mind and decided to no longer contribute to her "my-way-or-the-highway" policy.

I was leaving the next day and wanted to go next door to say goodbye to my friend Virgil. Knowing he would no longer be right next door brought a lump to my throat. I wanted to thank him for everything.

In the neighborhood, it was common knowledge what qualities my parents were missing. The Hess' home was my safe haven and my welcome over there lessened the severity of what took place at home. A lot of my free time growing up was spent with Virgil. He was eight years older and his friendship soothed my loneliness. The age gap didn't matter. I know God placed him there to save my sanity, and to fill in the missing link of a big brother and confidant.

We were similar outcasts, and grew inseparable. He was lonely like me and we just clicked. He was my best friend, and best friends tolerate whatever no one else wants to. Virgil had a genius-level mentality. He inspired me to strive and achieve beyond my own expectations and made me feel important. Mrs. Hess accepted me for who I was, and gave me a feeling of belonging. She appreciated my friendship with her son. Her open armed hugs were so important to me. Virgil had what I was longing to have—a happy home, and a mother who loved him just as he was. Virgil's mom cooked regular meals. Mom rarely cooked . . . maybe once a week. Stewart meals were chosen from a mile-high stack of Swanson's TV dinners. When we all had our fill of fried chicken with the dry brownie in the foil tins, it was either takeout Dad brought home for a typical 8:30 dinner time, or we'd cruise to whatever restaurant that might still be open.

My cravings for home-cooked food usually lured me over to the Hess' house right about what a normal dinner time should be. My hunger pangs anticipated savoring every morsel of those dinners, and my teenage bottomless pit of a stomach indulged in the ample supply of junk food that was never stocked in our own kitchen.

Virgil and I were competitive athletes, and we kept an ongoing tally of who won whatever game we played. His unique sense of humor made wiffle ball, flag football, and croquet unforgettable, and the highlight of my days. He was the one who encouraged me to try and find myself; the only one who gave me permission to just be me.

I relied on his positive reassurance to drown out Mother yelling her degrading comments at me in front of everyone. It all started with my participation in the annual all-city spelling bee. From the seventh grade through the ninth grade, I had found it nearly impossible to concentrate on winning with her harassment adding to my nervousness.

She'd rant so everyone could hear, "How could you miss that word? Really? It wasn't that hard. And you call yourself a Stewart?"

It didn't stop there. Sports was my passion. Baseball and basketball were an outlet for me. I could have been a most valuable player if Mom wasn't there, but when she showed up, her criticism did too.

She'd shout, "I can't believe you struck out." "That was an easy shot. Anyone else could have made that one." "You failed your team. How despicable."

It put a damper on even the coaches. I am surprised she wasn't escorted out. It would have been more supportive of her if she'd never attended at all.

It was unpredictable when Mother would come and make a complete fool out of herself. She'd usually introduce herself to the coach as the mother of that "fantastic player with so much potential."

One day, I wasn't feeling well, but there was no way I was going to miss my first practice with the varsity basketball team. And, there was no way I was going to stay home with Mother. I felt important being one of the only three seventh graders chosen out of all who tried out.

Being tactful and staying on the sidelines was not my mother's way. During the middle of a scrimmage, she boldly shot straight out toward our coach, Mr. Walker.

He blew his whistle so the players would not run her down. Mom had everyone's attention—just the way she liked it. "Hello, Coach Walker, I am Betty Lou Stewart, Tom's mother. Tom was not feeling well this morning, so I brought some Tums for his tummy."

The players were close enough to overhear what she said. I could have died. Coach Walker crossed his arms. From his face, I couldn't tell if he was amused or not. From the looks of it, I don't think he could help himself. "Well, well, well, player number 53, Tommy Tums." Then he chuckled sarcastically, "Hey, Mrs. Stewart, I actually think I could use some Tums for myself. My sissy team is playing so poorly, they are giving me nothing but indigestion." Hounded by the laughter, my new label became my worst nightmare: "Tommy Tums."

After so many variations of humiliation from an early age, I was basically immune to embarrassment. Not sure if that is a good thing, or if it made me oblivious.

Although, there was one thing that did embarrass me. Our family vehicle. It was a huge monster of a thing. Our mustard-colored Suburban, named after the movie Chitty Chitty Bang Bang. But Matt and I gave that gas-guzzling jalopy its well-earned, rhyming nickname—starting with the letter "s" in place of the letter "c." It wasn't the coolest vehicle for teenage boys to drive around and try to pick up chicks with. That's for sure. Either way, no matter how embarrassing the yellow bomb was, it was useful as my getaway car if Mother's mood happened to flare up.

Whenever possible, my other escape place was down in our basement. I'd head towards my place of solace away from the no-privacy zone upstairs. I claimed asylum down there, where I secluded myself from my family's issues. The basement became my sanctuary for studying, reading, journaling, and praying. I reserved one side of the Ping-Pong table as my workstation, where I laid out my schoolwork. On the opposite side of the torn Ping-Pong net sat stacks and stacks of my assignments and tests I held on to—accumulated since seventh grade. I lined them up perfectly adjacent to each other, collated by grade, and then by class. Nothing less than all A's—just as Mother demanded. My GPA was Mother's delight. I saw my performance of academics more like me as the lead dummy in her puppet show, with Betty Lou starring as the ventriloquist. Humoring her was purely the way that it was. I am extremely grateful how God blessed me with my intellect, but I did have to question the personality He gave my very strong-willed Norwegian mother. God revealed revelations and answered prayers sitting at the Ping-Pong table. I felt very close to Him down there. I could be still and feel genuinely loved as His son . . . and sometimes pretend I wasn't hers.

Eerily, the basement also held some of my worst memories. Just like that . . . the visions would come racing back. Flashes of what really happened down there. Seeing glimpses of his face in my face. I try to drown out his heavy breathing. *No! I'm free from him now. Free from his bondage.* Nobody knew, only the part of me that pretended nothing happened down there.

"Hey, Tom," Dad said through the door, "Mom and I are heading over to the church for a bit. We will be back in a while. Love you." I replied, "Okay, Dad. Love you."

I gave my parents a lot of credit for taking us to church every week. Whether it was a show for them or not, church was the most important social engagement we were never allowed to miss. I could have skipped over their hypocrisy about it all though.

Each Sunday at church, the good old Stewart family provided an opening act comedy scene. Mom strolled down the center aisle dragging us behind her, straight toward our special spot in the middle of the front row. Thirty minutes fashionably late was on time for my parents. Our matching little boy outfits complemented Mom's ensembles. She loved an audience and her fashion show moments in the spotlight. My Sunday morning breakfasts in the foyer of the church consisted of the humble pie I was force-fed, washed down with as much juice as I could gulp down. Dad thought it was ingenious to tuck away as many donuts as he could in his jacket for safekeeping. At least Mom had enough tact to not swipe anything from the church's silver service, as far as I knew.

I was startled by the doorbell. *Hmmm. That's strange. No one ever comes to the house. No one, except for one person . . . Bruce! It had to be him. That's his special ring of the bell . . .* I could feel the echo of the bell down to the soles of my feet. My body tensed up, and I sunk down in my chair. With my parents gone, I felt like a little kid left home alone. Praying he would go away, he insistently rang it again. *Oh, crap!*

No, Lord. Please! Please, make him go away.

I could just sit here, not move a muscle, and pretend that no one is home. But he probably knows I'm here. He always made sure to know where I was. Most likely, Bruce had watched my parents leave in Dad's car without me. He had probably waited for the opportune time to come and pay an unwelcome visit. I should have left for Virgil's sooner. *I know, I can hide below my window.* Bruce had a habit of stalking what he wanted, so walking around the house and peering in all the windows was not beyond him. *What should I do?*

I realized then that I needed to face him. *Enough is enough!* The bell rang one last time. There's no better time to do this. Giving myself a pep talk, *Okay courage, here we go. You took over when I faced Mother, I need you to take over again.* I shot up a quick prayer as I walked slowly to the door, *Lord, be with me.* I peeked through the peephole, and there he stood. I was right, it was Bruce. He looked like his usual frumpy self. Trying to appear calm, I opened the door, keeping the opening narrow by planting my size thirteen foot as a doorstop behind the door. He looked at me with a blank expression, but said nothing. We had the same competitive chip on both of our shoulders, and stared each other down.

I winced as I looked at the man standing in front of me. I wanted to lash out at him and say the worst words I could think of, but keeping it cordial was a better idea, "Hey," even though many far worse words came to mind. He nodded once, as he eased forward to invite himself in. My foot stayed put, keeping the door where it was. I attempted to detour him with, "I was just heading over to Virgil's house."

Bruce paused with a predictable sigh. Annoyed, he waited for me to open the door. He was like the incessant bully who had taken so much more from me than just my lunch money.

Bruce was not getting his customary welcome. He was also not receiving his on-cue compliance from me that he had become so used to. I cringed at the memory of my stolen decade as his homosexual sex slave.

Irritated, he had the gall to push his body against the door to try and secure his leverage by inserting his foot across the threshold as a wedge.

I stood firm. Pulling together all of the courage I never knew I had before, I boldly said, "Bruce . . . No!"

But Bruce was not accepting my "No." I had never experienced how he would respond when he didn't get what he wanted. His scowl deepened and he attempted to barge through.

As strange as it sounds, confronting my mother earlier had uncovered some buried brave in me. Even though she sided with Bruce, for me to finally stand up for myself was huge. But having it happen for me twice in one day was miraculous. I never thought I'd have any nerve at all.

"Bruce!" I yelled. "No more. I am done! You will not get near me again. You need to go away for good and leave me alone."

We glared at each other without flinching. Suddenly, panic rose up in me as his gun came to mind. My heart raced when I feared that he might have had it in the back of his pants.

No sooner than an instant did I feel the pressure of his foot against my foot lessening. Stepping back, without a sound, he made sure I saw his grimace of displeasure before turning his back on me. *Thank you, Lord, his gun is not back there.* I watched him leave with his posture slouched and his feet dragging down the driveway.

Shaking like crazy, all I wanted to do was yell at him—*"Why did you do this to me?"* But I quickly shut and locked the door. It was confusing. Bruce didn't seem to be angry—just disappointed, in a pouty kind of way. Strange, at the same time, I felt like crying. *Why in the world would I feel sad?*

Then, delayed regret hit me the same way it did that morning when I confronted Mother. I relived the same remorse: *How dare I insult Bruce like that?* How can two people who had used me and hurt me both make me feel as if I'm the bad guy? I tried to make sense of it, but my thoughts were all jumbled. *What's wrong with me?*

Outside, I heard my parents' car pull up. *They must have passed Bruce walking back down to his parents' house.* As the car doors slammed, I hurried to my room before they entered. Mother was the last person I needed to see.

Frazzled, thinking about what just happened had me fretting the worst; just as he intended. Come to think of it, he warned if I told anyone. *As far as he knows, I hadn't.* Mother's pride alone would keep her mouth shut tight about any of it. *I think we are safe.* In my mind, I replayed the pitiful expression on his face. In a disturbing way, it felt as if I had just broken up with him. Weird. I lay on my bed trying to get a grip. *Why did it bother me so much about Bruce walking away the way he did? Why do I feel like I betrayed him?*

Dad's footsteps came down the hall and he knocked on my door. He cracked it open and asked, "Tom, we saw Bruce coming out of our driveway and walking down the street towards his parents' house. Is everything okay? He didn't even look up when we waved. Mom is really concerned about him. She thought you might have said something to him." Being so irritated with Mother, I had to hold back responding how I really felt. My body seized as if all the blood rushed out of me; her bias toward her precious Bruce still had the power to hurt me. Of course, I knew what was smoldering underneath Mom's comments—my forbidden truth. I shrugged as he shrugged, and he shut the door.

Wrapping my head around what happened today—my face-to-face with Mother gave me the guts for my face-to-face with Bruce. An unfamiliar feeling of pride warmed me. Not the Stewart kind of pride, but a much-needed self-esteem boost of healthy pride. Maybe I owed Mom a big, huge thank-you for disappointing me. I used that to take a stand, and it made me feel as if I had slugged that bully right in the face!

FIVE

SCOUT LEADER'S PET

LATE THAT AFTERNOON, I mulled over my conflicted feelings. *What's the matter with me? Why do I feel so guilty about making Bruce feel bad?* He had used and abused me for more than half of my life.

Then I remember an incident we had talked about in one of my classes after a local teenage girl had been kidnapped. Walking home from school, she was pulled into a van, repeatedly raped, and then held captive for a week before being released.

Her reaction to the incident was not what people expected. *What did the teacher say she showed signs of? Didn't it start with an S?* Grabbing my encyclopedia, I thumbed through, panning the words of *sickness . . . symptoms . . . syndrome. That's it.* I read down the listings under syndrome when I came to what was called Stockholm syndrome. I read:

> A psychological response wherein a captive begins to identify closely with his or her captors, as well as with their agenda and demands. Psychologists who have studied the syndrome believe that the bond is initially created when a captor threatens a captive's life, deliberates, and then chooses not to kill the captive. The captive's relief at the removal of the death threat is transposed into feelings of gratitude toward the captor for giving him or her life . . . it takes only a few days for this bond to cement, proving that, early on, the victim's desire to survive trumps the urge to hate the person who created the situation. The

41

survival instinct is at the heart of the Stockholm syndrome. Victims live in enforced dependence and interpret rare or small acts of kindness in the midst of horrible conditions as good treatment. They often become hypervigilant to the needs and demands of their captors, making psychological links between the captors' happiness and their own. The syndrome is marked not only by a positive bond between captive and captor but also by a negative attitude on behalf of the captive toward authorities who threaten the captor-captive relationship.[1]

Did I have something like that? Compassion came easy for me. I was a natural at consoling others. It wasn't something taught to me by my parents, or even learned by their example, that's for sure. *What did Bruce's abuse do to me that Mom's didn't?* In my eyes, they were the same. *Could I have developed a traumatic bond with Bruce? That's crazy! What would people think? I can't tell anyone that.*

When I first heard the story of the kidnapped girl, I was fascinated. I now understood why and could relate some. Even though the girl's abuse lasted only for a week, she developed bonded feelings for her kidnapper. I was starting to put the pieces of my own life together. *But why didn't I feel the same way towards Mom?* I've always felt caught between Bruce's brainwashing and Mom's mind control. I was a victim to both, and damaged by both. They had done a number on me for sure. If I can just figure this out, maybe I could figure myself out. *Maybe someday.*

Bruce was sixteen when I met him. I was six. He lived with his parents in the white daylight rambler, with a one-car garage down at the end of my street, just left of the street sign at Dash Point Boulevard.

I could see it from my driveway, but often wished I couldn't, as it was one of the most vivid triggers of torment, besides my own home.

As far back as I can remember, Virgil, my brother, and I played our triple-play jump shots on the basketball court down the street. The

---

[1] Laura Lambert, "Stockholm Syndrome," *Encyclopaedia Brittanica*, www.britannica.com

academic agenda Mom set for me was so overloaded, it left little time for friends. So, I wanted to be with Virgil as often as I could—outside and away from the Twilight Zone in the Stewart residence.

After Bruce moved in the neighborhood, he joined in on games to complete a team of two-on-two. It felt real cool having two older guys wanting to hang out with me. They were my mentors, and filled Dad's position while he spent much of his time at work.

Bruce soon joined in our laughter at Mom's sundown routine. She'd blare out an obnoxious, "Where are you?" that was amplified up and down the street through a megaphone. No kidding—she really did own a megaphone. She wanted to portray to the neighbors that she had concern for our whereabouts. She wasn't calling because dinner was ready, obviously. It was our five-minute warning call to come home before she'd put her foot down. If we didn't report for duty within that five minutes, the door would be locked. No exceptions. Pretending I didn't hear her had resulted in many nights of sleepovers on the Hess' living room floor. A much better option than having to go back to a complete lockdown with Sargent Stewart on duty. *No, thank you. I thank God for Virgil and his family.*

I would say that I was grateful to be blessed with athleticism. I am not sure what I would have done if I hadn't had a full sports schedule to occupy me. It was my excuse to not be around the two people who wore me out more than any sport could.

More than anything, being an athlete counteracted the sissy harassment I got from playing the viola that Mom made my brother and me play. I am sure she wanted us to be famous with our matching instruments and matching black tuxedos with bow ties.

After hanging around the other "band geeks" for a while, I decided they weren't so different from me. They didn't tease me all the time like the other kids. I was proud to call them my friends, and proud to be called a "geek" right along with them. I will admit, I didn't think being in the Meeker Junior High orchestra would be something I would like, but playing in my first concert was incredible. We "geeks" sounded great together on stage. Unfortunately, the "bookworm" and "nerd" comments kept coming. I was taller than most boys, so that deflected the bullying a bit. But my ability to dodge Mom's attitude for so long that helped me overcome bullying like a pro.

I gritted my teeth each time she played barber; grabbing the scissors, in her attempt to chop my hair . . . I would say that butchering it was more like it. The always-crooked bowl cuts she gave me left me wide open for more teasing, until the next time my grown-out hair was up for grabs. And, her choice of glasses for me didn't help matters any. Cool wasn't anywhere close to what she chose, insisting on picking out the biggest, nerdiest glasses for me at the optical shop.

My concerns were eased when I saw Bruce proudly wearing his glasses; I felt mine weren't so nerdy after all. But it was the day that Bruce walked up the street; all decked out in his Scout uniform, that really impressed me. He looked sharp—reminding me of a soldier in a military uniform. All those cool badges of accomplishments, I wanted that too. And, so did Betty Lou. It was one more grand opportunity to shine the spotlight on her distinguished Stewart boy.

Bruce's mom was the secretary of his troop. Not that I wanted Mom to be anywhere involved with me, but I was envious of Bruce . . . downright jealous that he could be proud of his mom and even want to have her around.

Scouts appeared to me as a father and son activity, and I really wanted to do it with my dad. When Dad was a boy, he started out as a Cub Scout, went on to Boy Scouts, and earned the honor of Eagle Scout. That's what I wanted to do. I hoped Dad would get involved and participate with me and be my dad in more ways than by name only.

I begged Bruce to tell me how I could join. He told me, "Keep an eye out for the fliers going around the school when it begins in the fall. You would start out in Cub Scouts, just like your dad and I did." On the first day of third grade, my only desire was to seek out and find what Bruce was talking about. There it was—the 'Join the Cub Scouts' flier. *Bruce was right. He is so smart.* It said that boys are eligible to join at age seven. *Yay! I was seven, almost eight.* I stuffed the flier in my backpack, and couldn't wait to bring it home to show my parents. Well, at least my dad, anyway. Hoping my parents would say yes, I wanted this more than anything.

Impatiently, I waited for Dad to come home from work so I could show him first. I didn't dare ask Mom just yet. It seemed like I was waiting forever. I tried my best to stay calm when I heard him unlock the front door. I gave him a little bit of time to settle in, and then excitedly approached him as he sat in his chair.

As he glanced over the flier, he looked pleased. "Oh, this brings back memories, Tom. So, you want to join Cub Scouts?" Dad looked over at me as if taking my measure. "Are you ready to take on this responsibility?"

Hardly able to contain myself, I said, "Yes, Dad, more than anything ever in my whole entire life . . . please!" I wanted to feel important and mature, especially in Bruce's eyes. I was happy Dad seemed interested.

When Mom saw the flier, she snatched it up. I wasn't surprised at her butting in. Putting a damper on my moment, she insisted, "You had better go into this at full speed and with flying colors, Tom, or don't go in at all. And, it had better not interfere with your school work, sports, church, or your viola practice."

I had learned how to use her fire as fuel for me to try harder and get ahead—and there was sure a lot of it. Maybe part of Dad's sudden interest was a spiteful challenge against Mother. Maybe another reason to get away from home? Or, maybe he coveted the pseudo-father position Bruce had so kindly taken in his place? Despite the reaction from my parents, it was Bruce who influenced me to go for it. He was the one who gave me all the confidence I needed. He was raring to teach me and guide me, and he was right there to take me all the way.

I had daydreams of one day becoming an Eagle Scout . . . just like Bruce. Dad was one too, but there was something more intriguing about Bruce. He coached me on what it meant to be a Scout and how I should present myself as such.

The first meeting was scheduled for Tuesday, October 6—the same day as my eighth birthday. *This will be the best birthday I have ever had.* It gave me four weeks to prepare before our first pack meeting. Bruce seemed thrilled with my interest. He said that my enthusiasm reminded him of himself when he was my age. He said that he wanted to see me succeed, and was going to help me every step of the way.

We started with the book knowledge that I needed to memorize to become a new Cub Scout. "Now Tom," Bruce stressed, "This is going to be hard work, but I know you can do it. It's been so long since I have had to recite anything from the Cub Scouts, we can review together."

We started out simple. He read, "The first rank that every boy earns when entering the Cub Scouting Program is the Bobcat rank. These requirements are meant to demonstrate that the boy is making a commitment of participating in the Scout program."

"Tom, are you ready to be a Bobcat?"

I could barely contain myself. "Yes, I am."

"Tom, I want to remind you that when you are in the presence of a superior, you are to address him as 'Sir.'"

No matter what kind it was, I gladly absorbed the long overdue attention I was getting from Bruce.

"Oh, I'm sorry, Sir. Yes, Sir."

Saying, "Yes, Sir" to Bruce came naturally.

"I am going to read the Bobcat rank requirements, Tom, and I want you to repeat after me. You will need to memorize each of these and recite them by heart. Are you prepared to do this?"

"Yes, Sir, I can do this."

Bruce proceeded to read the Scout Oath for Cub Scouts and Boy Scouts:

"On my honor, I will do my best

To do my duty to God and my Country and to obey the Scout Law; To help other people at all times;

To keep myself physically strong, mentally awake, and morally straight."

"Tom, here is the Scout Law. I'm sure all twelve of the elements will be easy for you since you already possess these qualities as it stands. Are you ready?" He read, "A Scout is: trustworthy, loyal, helpful, friendly, courteous, kind, obedient, cheerful, thrifty, brave, clean, and reverent."

"See what I mean, Tom. You rock! I feel honored to be your teacher. Thank you for being a great student."

Next, Bruce said, "So, I am sure you have seen the Cub Scout Sign before, right?" I nodded. "Of course, you have, Tom—I knew it. I'm impressed. See how your fingers look like a wolf's ear ready to listen?"

"Wow, Bruce, that's cool. Thank you," smiling from my wolf's ear to wolf's ear.

"Time for the Cub Scout Handshake. Please come here and stand in front of me, Tom."

After we'd practiced the handshake, I proudly said, "Okay, I think I got it, Sir."

This is going to be awesome! "This is like another kind of language, right, Sir?

"And now for the Cub Scout Motto. Do you happen to know what the motto is, Tom?"

"No. Sorry, Sir."

"It is, 'Do Your Best.'"

"Do Your Best. Yes. I will do my best, Sir. Thank you, Sir."

"I know you will, Tom."

"And, finally, the Cub Scout Salute. Just like you would salute in the military. Saluting is showing your respect to their authority. Just like you are expected to salute the flag, showing you are proud of your country."

Bruce's instruction made me feel like an instant adult. No one had ever taken so much interest in what I wanted before. Bruce was like my superhero from a comic book.

He was always on top of reminding me over and over again to live by the Scout Law and Scout Motto. He said, "These are not traits for just the Scouts, but we should live life this way—to be moral and ethical, upstanding citizens."

I already knew how important it was for me to follow rules and respect others, but with Bruce stressing what he expected from me, I tried that much harder to be the best Scout possible. He showed me by his example how to do it, and I respected him greatly.

If it was my dad who coached me to do what Bruce did, I might have humored him because he was my dad, but I may not have taken it as seriously.

Starved for attention, I sought out approval wherever I could get it. Bruce, who was somewhat of a loner like me, gave me what I was missing. I worked hard to be recognized and favored in all areas of my life. I set out to be teacher's pet, coach's pet, and pastor's pet. Heck, I was even the lunch lady's pet. In doing so, it always got me a second helping for free!

Bruce built up my missing self-esteem. All I had known about myself up to that point was how to try to make Mom happy. It didn't matter if I was happy. I was like a robot and my "Yes, Mother" skipped like a broken record, but never played the tune I would have chosen. I just wanted to be a kid for once. But I also wanted to be loved, needed, and feel important.

Trying my hardest to live up to being that perfect son she wanted, I sacrificed Saturday after Saturday to accompany Mom on her three-hour-long hair appointments—cut, color, roller, and dry. I sat patiently as if there was no other place I would rather be. I also followed her to doctor appointments, eye doctor appointments, chiropractor appointments, and even to get her manicures.

Then, my "Yes, Mother" days would end with me pushing the heavy cart at the local dark and dusty Prairie Market supermarket. It was a long process to get to the checkout line. I'd grab the greasy black marking pens in the brown cardboard box by the front door, and, carry it with me to handwrite the shelf price on every item down each aisle. It didn't feel like a typical grocery store, it felt more like a warehouse. I'm surprised Mother chose this bag-your-own and carry out-your-own groceries type of store. She was so used to being catered to . . . I guess that's why I was there. I must have been in training to be a doting husband someday.

When I met other moms, I realized my own mom wasn't one of those nurturing types. She was the one who expected to be nurtured—more like catered to. I was just the one to do it for her. Spoiled with ice packs for her eyes, along with a delicious breakfast expected to be served to her in bed every weekend by no other than Tommy.

Her strange companionship needs wore me out. But I knew I was to always respect her. I waited and waited for some appreciation in return for my loyalty. Feeling like the Energizer Bunny, I kept going and going. Always on standby—on high alert for a simple, "Thank you," or even an "I'm proud of you."

Even then, I had the feeling her attachment to me wasn't healthy, and even a little bit creepy. Mother would plan long private lunches on the patio in the summer with just me, calling it our special mother/son bonding time.

Having lunch with Mom was not the strange part, but her sitting so uncomfortably close to me was. She told me once, "I wish Dad were more like you." It felt as if she was coming on to me in some way.

So, joining Cub Scouts was an offer I jumped at. I was looking forward to feeling and acting like a normal kid. I wanted to do kid stuff, and maybe even get dirty like other kids. I wanted to be anything but perfect for once.

Boy, was I surprised when Dad volunteered to be my Cubmaster that first year. Bruce didn't seem to be happy about it. His face drooped when Dad and I told him the news. He was obviously disappointed and I wondered why. I thought he would be happy about it. Bruce had always made it a point to win over my parents by buying them gifts at Christmas, birthdays, and just because. Which is why Bruce probably was the only person outside of our own family who was ever allowed in our private penitentiary of a home.

Trying on my new uniform for the first time, I felt proud. On den meeting days, I was relieved to be free from the matching Stewart plaids or those comical orange terry cloth socks she always made us wear. The color was so bright, they practically glowed in the dark under my high-water pants.

Mother despised doing laundry, and I rarely had clean clothes. Lucky for me, a clean and pressed uniform was mandatory for each meeting, so she had to do laundry. It was nice not to have to rummage through my dirty clothes hamper on those days to find something clean.

I couldn't wait to learn which merit badges I'd start working toward first. I had a long way to go before I graduated to a sash filled with all what Bruce had earned. The morning of my birthday came, and I almost forgot. *Happy Birthday to me!* Since my brother's birthday was also in October, Mom just combined them both, smack dab in the middle of each other. I didn't think it was fair for either of us. So, having my first Cub Scout meeting on my birthday at least made it a special day.

It was cool to step out of my house and head off to school in my uniform. The bus driver, my teacher, my P.E. teacher, the lunch lady, the recess teacher, and even the janitor said how good I looked. I felt so grown up and official. My birthday didn't matter, though my class sang me the *'Happy Birthday'* song, and attempted to spank me on recess. The playground lady made sure that didn't happen. I guess I was the playground teacher's pet too.

Squirming in my seat, it was coming up on 3:00 p.m., everything felt as if it was going in slow motion. *Come on . . . ring bell, ring!*

I ran home as fast as I could, I did my homework, and was ready to go by 3:45. All this waiting was driving me crazy. All I wanted for my birthday was for the time to go faster.

I didn't want to forget my handbook and cap. This would be a great time to go over my Scout Oath and Scout Law to make sure I have it down. *I wouldn't want to let Bruce down.* Time was ticking slowly as I stared out the window reciting what I remembered. I was a little nervous, not knowing what to expect, but *I've got Bruce. He's got me covered. He always does.* Bruce; already an accomplished Eagle Scout, was dubbed to be an assistant to our pack. Even though he was not eighteen quite yet, the rules were bent since he was truly a seasoned Scout.

I wanted to follow in his shadow—right behind him as Scout leader's pet. He had promised me he would do whatever it took to help me earn my merit badges—I believed him. Never in a million years could I have realized then what that would come to mean.

We met at the activity club about two miles away from home, quite a way to walk if I didn't have a ride. Since Mom's reliability was uncertain and Dad had to rush straight to the pack meeting directly from work, Bruce took it upon himself to swing by and pick me up whenever needed. Since Mom didn't work, I found it kind of odd how she was rarely ever home after school we got off the bus. When she did come home, her hands were never empty. Full of who knows what. She seemed exasperated by her hard day's shopping . . . or could it have been shoplifting? It was always a mystery as to how she acquired all her stuff. Her not being home, I didn't know if she was trying to force us to appreciate her by keeping us locked but without a key on purpose? The covered patio in between the garage and house became our sheltered, homework area until she decided to come back home. Of course, she was too tired to cook dinner when she did, but never too tired to run down her list of Tommy's to-do-for-Mom list. I was programmed perfectly to cater to Betty Lou's every whim. Bruce knew I was one of those latchkey kids, just one without a key. He also knew I was lonely. He told me, "You can always count on me for anything. I'll be here for you—whatever you need, Tom."

It's him! He's here! I didn't want to do anything wrong by him, so I just waited to see what he was going to do. I didn't know if I was supposed to wait for his honk, or if he was going to get out and come up to the front door. *Front door it is.* He had one arm behind his back, and he shut the door with the other. He rang the bell in a neat way—two quick, then one long buzz. Mother answered the door, while I gathered my belongings. I heard him say, "Well, hello Mrs. Stewart, how are you today? Did you do something new with your hair?" Then, he pulled out what was behind his back. A pretty bouquet of flowers—just for her. His smile and flattery were about as thick as his glasses were.

Basking in his compliments, Mom blushed, and said, "Thank you for the flowers. That was very nice of you." He sure knew how to charm. It worked every time. Mom was usually in a constant state of irritation; especially with Dad, but when I saw her face light up and her mood calm down, it felt like a breath of fresh air to me. Her cheerful glow resulted in a brief ceasefire in the entryway. I was impressed how Bruce could break through her barrier. He was good! Really good.

I was just a boy. He gave me a sense of security I had never known. I trusted him. He had everything covered and under control. I felt really taken care of. And, wow, if he could make my mom happy, he was special!

Feeling handsome, I was proud to come to the door and show Bruce the new me, all dressed up in my uniform. With my scarf perfectly adjusted, I grabbed my cap, and squeezed by Mom. Still soaking up her moment, I kissed her on the cheek, and chanted the usual, "Love you."

Bruce said to her, "I'm not sure what time we will get home, Mrs. Stewart. I would like to review a few things with Tom afterwards; of course, if that is okay with you, ma'am?" She nodded and waved, then shut the door.

Side by side, the Eagle Scout was escorting his trainee Scout. "Boy, you look snazzy in your new uniform, Tom," he said. "You will start earning your skill awards in no time."

I smiled and placed my cap firmly on my head, thinking, *I am so lucky to have Bruce as my friend.*

SIX

HOW COULD I?

THIS IS REAL cool. The afternoon was sunny as Bruce drove down Marine View Drive. I reached up to pull the visor down; Bruce's hand was right there to help me lower it. I needed it not only to block out the sun, I wanted to see how "snazzy," as Bruce put it, I looked.

"Make sure the door is locked," Bruce reminded me.

Nope, it wasn't. So, I clicked it down with my elbow, feeling sly. At the stop sign, he glanced in his rearview mirror; and then over at me, eagerly telling me, "Let's turn on some tunes." He turned the radio dial on, and started rocking out to some music that he said sounded "dynamite."

"Yeah, that's dynamite, all right," I said. I wasn't real sure what we were listening to, but wanted to be just like Bruce. Too bad he hadn't picked me up earlier. It would have been great to roll the windows down and cruise around a little while longer—even if it was cold. I wouldn't have cared if I froze. All those gauges on the dash looked like a flashy pinball machine. *I can't wait to learn how to use a compass like Bruce has there stuck on the dashboard.* The little, round stick-on clock read 4:35. *Great, we still have some time to ride around.* Bruce was in a very happy mood and asked, "Are you having a good birthday so far?"

I felt giddy and said, "Yes, thank you, Bruce." Shocked by what just came out of my mouth, I looked down and said, "Oops, sorry, I know I am supposed to call you 'Sir' when in uniform, right?"

In a reassuring voice, he said, "Tom, when it is just the two of us, you can always call me Bruce, but that stays between us, okay?" He pulled his left hand off the steering wheel, crossed over his right, and flew a high-five my way. *This is the most fun I think I've had . . . ever!*

"We have about twenty minutes to spare, Tom. I have a surprise for you for your birthday." He swung around to park in front of a burger and fry joint called 'Frisco Freeze.' They had the best shakes.

I sat up in my seat and I looked him in the eyes with a grin so wide. "I love this place Bruce. It is my favorite!"

"What flavor of milkshake would you like, Tom?"

I chose chocolate; he ordered strawberry. We sat in his truck and gulped them down to almost the very last slurp. My teeth were chattering. "Ugh, brain freeze at Frisco Freeze!"

Bruce snorted, and almost spit out what was left in his mouth.

We both just laughed and laughed like great chums.

Gasping in between my belly laughs, I blurted out, "Thank you for the shake." Bruce wiped his mouth off from his own fit of laughter and bellowed, "I just want to make my Prize Scout happy." I couldn't believe it. *Did he just say I am his Prize Scout?*

Then he laid his right hand on my left knee. I look up at him—he was watching me as if he was in a trance. I glanced away, and back at him still zoning in on me. I wanted to ask him, "Are you okay?" but I didn't.

He exhaled and seemed to snap out of it. He asked me, "Ready to go?" Then, he gave my knee a little squeeze.

I didn't think anything of it. It was kind of like a good buddy pat on the back thing, like my dad or grandpa would do. I was happy. *No doubt about it. This is my best birthday yet.*

We arrived at the meeting place, joining up with the Cub Scout pack. Dad's car was already parked near the front, so we parked right next to it. Bruce walked beside me with his hand on my back toward the other boys who were congregating by the front door. The ones who didn't know Bruce assumed he must be one of the leaders, so they waited for his okay to go inside. I felt special being the chosen one with him. I had never felt popular before.

Dad was waiting at the podium, wearing his old Boy Scout uniform. I had never seen him in it before. It still fit him. *Cool, my dad is Cubmaster, and Bruce is Den Chief.* Dad cued all of us to gather together up near the stage. The boys were a little rowdy, so Bruce corralled them all to listen. Dad introduced himself to the boys who did not know him yet.

The meeting began with an official roll call, followed by a meet and greet for the boys who didn't know each other.

Dad then introduced Bruce. He welcomed each boy with a firm handshake, and made sure each new Cub Scout knew the basics.

Dad announced how our pack meetings would go. "We will start out with a prayer for the day, followed by a formal opening flag ceremony. Bruce, please demonstrate."

I watched Bruce as he demonstrated, thinking, *He's a good teacher.* Dad said, "The pack will sing a song through the flag ceremony and finish off with the Cub Scout Promise when the flags come to a halt. We will then discuss any unfinished business, and upcoming events. When it comes time, we will present your earned skill awards. Then it will be time for the pack activities to begin. We will end with a closing prayer, reciting our Scout Oath and Scout Law, followed by the closing flag ceremony."

At this meeting, we went through the handbook and Dad explained what Cub Scouts was all about, the ranks, and how to climb.

This definitely is my thing. It's going to take a lot of work, but I'm in! Dad gestured Bruce to proceed with the closing flag ceremony, and Bruce nudged me to help him. *I feel very honored—and cool at the same time.*

We finished up our meeting with all the Scouts reciting the Scout Oath in sync with each other: "On my honor . . ."

With my first official pack meeting under my shiny belt, I politely tapped my dad's shoulder, and let him know I would be riding home with Bruce. Walking about ten feet tall next to my superior—my "Sir"—I assumed the shotgun position in his truck again, hoping all the other boys were watching me get in.

The sky-high wishes I had for my Scouting adventure birthday were coming true, thanks to Bruce. As Bruce pulled out of the parking lot,

I never could have imagined that his destination would take me on a detour to a place where my childhood would no longer be mine.

It's getting dark. The time on the round stick-on clock is 6:39. I reach over to turn the radio back on so we could rock out like we did on the way. But Bruce quickly shuts it off. His mood seems different and a little bit strange. Suddenly worried, I ask, "Did I do something wrong, Sir?" The last thing I would ever want to do is make Bruce mad. He shakes his head, *no.* I am so used to the unpredictable mood shifts with Mom, I know just what to do . . . lay low and keep quiet. Unexpectedly, he turns the steering wheel and we swerve off the main drag, making the two empty milkshake cups roll around on the floor. With my feet playing goalie, I'm trying to keep what drips are left in the cups from spilling all over the floor. He is driving along some unpaved side streets where I had never been before. His speed is very slow and is coasting at a stop-and-go pace. Him tapping on his brakes seems like he is searching for some place in particular.

The compass on the dash is bouncing around from all the bumps and potholes. *I feel like he's taking me on my first Cub Scout off-road adventure.* He slows the truck to a stop in the middle of a street. He leans way over toward me to open the glove box and fumbles for something. I stay quiet. He's being a little creepy and it's freaking me out, like when Mom's acting strange. His sweaty armpit is in my face. The strong smell of his deodorant mixed with his icky odor gag me a little. I sink down in my seat so I don't smother in his shirt. *Oh, that's what he was looking for . . . a map.* He shifts back over to his own seat, centers himself, and studies the map. Then we start driving up a steep hill. It is getting dark, so he needs to flip on the overhead dome light. He glances down to his map, and back up to see where he is heading. *Should I ask him where we are going? He did tell Mom he wanted to review a few things with me after the meeting, so I think that's what we're going to do.*

Bruce pulls his truck over to the side of the road. It was like out in the middle of nowhere. The stick-on clock reads 6:47.

He moves the gearshift to the middle and then from side to side. The truck kind of sways from front to back until he firmly pulls out the emergency brake to lock it in place. He shuts the ignition to off, slides the overhead dome light to the off position, and then turns off the headlights. It's darker now.

I bend down to the floor where my feet are still holding the cups in place to keep them from making a mess. *It is hard to see without the dome light.* I feel his hand grab my leg. I shudder when his arm starts to move over my lap, and his elbow crosses over my privates. That's what Mom taught me to call them. *That tickles!* He must be trying to boost himself up. His arm grazes back over my lap giving me the same tickling feeling over my privates again. *I hope he doesn't scratch himself on my belt.* He reaches over me one more time to pull the lever that reclines my seat back. *I'm sure he will have enough room to get himself up now.*

Bruce whispers, "Tom, I need you to lie down." He helps to guide me backward on the reclined seat. The squeaky praise in his voice sounds strange to me, "I am so proud of my Prize Scout, I'm going to give you a massage because you have worked so hard."

His gentle touch is something I've never felt before. My parents are anything but touchy-feely.

"Tom, you want a massage, right?"

"Yep."

Bruce grabs the bar in front of my seat and pulls it. My seat slides back fast, and abruptly stopped as far back as it can go. I can hear him rustle around on the floorboard down in front of me, and crumple the cups under my seat. "I need to squat down right here, Tom, so I can massage you better."

It's pitch dark now. *I would be scared if Bruce weren't here.* Reaching around my body with both of his arms, he hugs me tight. He rests his head on my tummy, but not hard enough to hurt. *I like Bruce's hugs, because I know how much he likes me. I would do anything for him. He's done so much for me.* His hands move back around and start massaging my chest. His massage is giving me chills and goose bumps.

"Tom, do you trust me?"

I again say, "Yep." He already knows I do. Mom has ground every single manner into my head, like always saying please and thank you, but to obey authority has always been at the very tippy top.

In a soft voice, Bruce tells me, "I'm going to adjust your belt buckle, Tom; it feels too tight." Click goes the brass buckle. "Oops, the button to your pants came undone too." He pauses and waits for a response from me.

I say nothing, thinking, *is this what massage therapists do? He sure knows how to give good massages. He should really be one.*

I feel the vibration as my zipper glides down. I'm unbuttoned and unzipped. *Good thing I put on clean underwear under my new uniform.* It was so dark, it wouldn't have mattered anyway. He tugs on my shirt to un-tuck it and reaches up underneath on my bare skin, sliding his hands from my neck down my chest to where my pants used to be buttoned.

It's kind of like playing doctor. *I've never played doctor before.*

Bruce reaches behind me and rubs me from the top of my spine all the way down to my pants, but doesn't stop there. He is now pulling my pants down.

He's pretty sneaky. He doesn't say anything and I don't either. All I can hear is him breathing heavy.

The massage continues around my hips. My body is now quivering. It is cold in the truck, but it's a different kind of quiver. His massage glides down my thighs to where my pants are binding me around my knees, and then he goes back up again.

I'm a little worried if he accidentally touches my privates, but it is Bruce after all, so I don't ask him why he is pulling my underwear down. I'm glad it's dark so Bruce doesn't see this weird look on my face.

I'm lying here bare naked.

Woah, Bruce is massaging me down there too. Tickles, goosebumps, shivers.

He made my privates stick straight up, standing at attention like I do to Bruce. *Oh, my gosh, should I ask him to stop? Nope, I don't tell my Scout leader what to do.*

I've felt myself down there before, but Mother's screaming voice echoes through my head, reminding me "Don't ever touch your privates."

But, this is different. He's my Scout leader, it must be okay. She doesn't have to find out. *I can keep a secret.*

All of a sudden, there's a strange feeling of . . . I don't know what. My muscles are so tense. He keeps going and going. *What is he doing?* He's not stopping.

I start to shake. I arch my back, and lift my hands up over my head and grab on to the top of the headrest.

Something's happening, something's happening. I'm panting so fast.

Then . . . *oh no, I feel like I need to pee. I can't hold it!* Bruce bolts his head back away from me, and I hear it bang on the dash. I can't see his face, but can hear him growling in disgust.

He yanks on the door handle, and swings it open to throw his head out the door to spit.

"Bleh! Nasty!" He gags. I gag listening to him gag. "What did you do that for, Tom? You peed all over my face!"

I want to sink down lower than I already am. *He is so mad. I am scared. I am so embarrassed.* I didn't mean to make him mad. "I'm sorry Bruce, I'm sorry, I'm sorry!"

He says nothing. He hovers over me to get himself out the door to slam it. I hear him spitting, over and over again. I stare out at the dark feeling ashamed. My heart races as I hear him rustling through the grass behind the truck. Then he tramps around to open the driver's side door. *I wish he'd shut the door quick,* the dome light is shining a spotlight on me. *I don't want him to see me.* Bruce turns the ignition on to start the truck. The dash light glows on my naked body. I look back and forth between him and my pulled down pants. He tells me, "Pull 'em up."

I nervously lift up my rear end and try to do what he says and "pull 'em up." Can't seem to get a grip. I manage to find my belt loops and tug them up far enough to button and zip, then click to close my belt. I don't bother tucking my shirt in, I can't see.

I disappointed Bruce and made him mad. He is going to hate me.

I reach down to grab for the lever to put the seat back up in its upright position. Bam! The seat hits me full blast in the back of the head. Reaching for my seat belt, I get it fastened, and stare forward to see Bruce's high beams light up in front of us. Bruce puts the truck in gear, and peels out on to the road. I cower down like a puppy that just got in trouble.

When I see streetlights on the side of the road, I know we must be heading back. I don't dare touch the radio dial this time. *I'm so stupid! Bruce probably wants to take back calling me his Prize Scout.* We come up to a four-way stop, and I now recognize the street we are on; we are near home. I glance over at him to see if he is still mad. *Yep,* he's still mad. His eyebrows look angry and his face not happy. The lights from the intersection we passed lit up the time on the stick-on clock. It now says 7:31. *I will tell my parents that Bruce helped me work on some new Cub Scout stuff like he told Mom he was going to do. I know I won't get in trouble for being this late since Mom already said it was okay. They don't need to know anything about Bruce giving me a massage, the playing doctor stuff, or any of the naked stuff. I will only say something if Bruce does.*

Bruce pulls into our driveway behind my parents' cars. He brakes the truck to a stop, rapidly shifts into reverse, and waits for me to get out. He is more than ready to get on out of there.

I get the hint, but I wait with a tight hold on the door handle; hoping he will finally say something . . . anything! Using my good manners, I break the silence and tell him, "Thank you for my birthday treat, and for picking me up and dropping me off."

Looking the other way, he only nods. As soon as I get out and step clear of his tires, he swiftly backs up, squeals to a half-stop, and almost peels out as he leaves. I stood there watching his tail lights; thinking, *I'm going to do whatever it takes to make Bruce happy.*

SEVEN

PRIZE SCOUT

I TUCK MY shirt back in and straighten my cap. *I don't want my parents to suspect anything. Oh no, I left my handbook in Bruce's truck. Maybe he will come back tomorrow and give it back to me. I sure hope so.*

I'm hoping they left the door unlocked for me. The kitchen light is on and I'm hungry. I would sure love to have one of my favorite peanut butter and mayo sandwiches. No, I better not. Not sure what kind of a look I have on my face. I might slip up and tell whoever is in the kitchen I have been playing doctor with Bruce.

Instead, I go down the hall as quietly as I can, and make it safe and sound to my bedroom. It kind of reminds me of playing hide-and-seek.

Oh, shoot. The floor's creaking and there are footsteps coming down the hall. I can't hide for long. I guess they found me.

"Knock, knock."

It's Mom and Dad, both of them.

I fib and say, "I'm changing." It wouldn't matter. Mom might come in anyway. Someone else's privacy is not one of her strong points.

Dad says, "Hey Tom, we just wanted to say 'Happy Birthday' and good night. Love you."

Phew, they're not coming in. I say back, "Thank you, and love you too."

"Oh, that was close," I whisper. I hate lying though. It makes me feel like there is a huge heavy rock on my chest until I tell the truth. I don't want to think about that right now. I undress down to just my underwear, and neatly hang my uniform on my clothes rack with my cap. *Perfect. If I had clean underwear, I'd change those too. The smell of Bruce's Old Spice is still stuck on me—and that might be just enough to give it away. It's probably best I tiptoe to the bathroom to wash the smell off. Yep, that's what I will do.*

I quietly open my door and head down to the bathroom. Turning on the light, I look in the mirror and see, *I look different.* Aiming for the center of the toilet bowl, I can't help but think what Bruce said about me peeing all over him. *Yuck! I'll try to make it up to him. Maybe we can play doctor again and I can do it right next time.* I search for a clean washcloth. I find one that's clean enough. Aw, this will do. Under the faucet, I roll the bar of soap in between my hands and the washcloth to lather it up. Then I pull down my underwear like Bruce did. *He was so sneaky about the way he did it. I need to hurry up and get back to my room before my parents hear me.* "Pull 'em up" like Bruce says is what I did.

The washcloth didn't get the smell off me, it must be stuck in my nose. Back in my bed, I turn out the lights. I'm tired, but wide awake at the same time. I see the moonlight peeking through a crack in the middle of the curtains. It's shining a streak on my bed.

I talked to God like I usually do. "Thank you for my day today, God. Thank you, God for my birthday today. Thank you, God, for my first pack meeting. Thank you, God for my friendship with Bruce. Please, God, help him not be mad at me. And, God, I don't know what I would do if he didn't like me anymore. Thank you, God."

The seemingly innocent game of chance Bruce played with me that night was just the start of what my next ten years would dish out.

Bruce's cleverness took ownership of me whenever he wanted to with a well-rehearsed routine of control. It was as if he had earned part of me, and was entitled to his prey.

This continued at least once a week for the next 520 weeks. He spent two years grooming me—then spent the next ten years manipulating me, and sexually abusing me. My life all seems like a hazy blur—except for what he did to me. I have all the proof that I participated in Scouts—stashed away behind my closet door. All the proof I went through the ranks, but have little memory of it. The pictures of what I have in my mind reveal the expensive price I paid for earning all those skill awards and merit badges, but I am the only one who can see what I see. The abuse surfaces in many ways. They catch me off guard, over and over again—visions, nightmares, and flashbacks. It's as if the devil was constantly hovering, waiting to dive in and devour; using Bruce as his demon pawn to have his way. This is my constant reality.

The morning after was weird. I walked off to school as usual, but with a bounce in my step. I was now eight and felt more grown up. Besides, I had an important mission. I had to get Bruce to like me again. I thought about it all the way to school, and the whole day through. I didn't pay much attention all day in class. At lunch, I hoped so hard he might come and have lunch with me. On the playground, I looked around wishing Bruce might pay me a visit through the chain-link fence. I couldn't stop thinking about it all the way home from school. Mom wasn't home again. Not like that was anything new. *Oh well, I'll sit out here and do my homework like I always do.*

Then I thought I heard his truck coming around the corner. Yes, there was Bruce's Scout. *Cool!* But he just sped by. *Oh . . . wait, he's backing up.* He must have seen me sitting there. My heart started to pound in excitement. He pulled into the driveway and rolled down his window. I'm whispering to myself, *please, please, please don't be mad anymore.*

He stepped out of his truck and slammed his door, but not a very hard slam, and walked toward me in his take-charge walk. The day was kind of sunny, but kind of not. So, his glasses that changed from clear to shaded were stuck in between. I couldn't tell if his eyes were mad or if his eyes were happy.

"Hi, Bruce," I said with a smile, hoping to get a smile out of him. He tipped his head with his typical, *hey*. "I've got your handbook at my house. I'll come back and we can work on Scout stuff."

I was so excited. Bruce seemed him same self again. I made sure he heard my anxious "See you later."

About forty-five minutes went by before Mom pulled up in our driveway. I had finished my homework in the nick of time.

When Mom stepped out of the truck, I was surprised to see no shopping bags in her hands. She walked by me and said, "Hi, Son, doing homework I see."

"Yes, Mother," I said. "I am going to wait right here. Bruce said he was going to stop by and help me with some Cub Scout stuff."

"Okay. You might as well go in the basement. That way you will have some privacy."

I was confused. But no one is allowed in our house. *What's going on with Mother? Did the flowers give her a crush on Bruce? No, she's married . . . that's just weird. Oh well, I don't care; he gets to come in.*

Twenty minutes, then thirty minutes passed by. *Where is Bruce?* Finally, I see him walk towards me up the driveway with my handbook in his hand. The little bit of sun that was out earlier went behind the clouds, so his glasses were now clear, and I could see his whole face. Not smiley, just okay.

"Why don't you get your stuff, Tom. I assume that your mom will let us go over what we need to do in your house, right?" I was so excited to tell him that Mom already said that we could. Not only was Bruce not mad anymore, Mom was letting him in the no-go zone. *This is another great day,* I told myself. I walked in the house, and he followed. I whispered to Bruce, "You should feel special to come past the front door. Nobody else has been that lucky. My mom must really like you."

Bruce just nodded. There was Mom; just around the corner in the kitchen, adding water to the flowers Bruce brought her the night before. She immediately smiled at Bruce and greeted him.

He said a very cheerful, "Hello, Mrs. Stewart," back to her.

"Hey, Mom, is it still okay if we go down in the basement to work on more Cub Scout stuff?" "Sure, absolutely," she told me, "I am going to go and lie down anyway."

I led Bruce towards the door to the basement and opened it. I let him know, "My dad won't be home for a while, Bruce, so we shouldn't be interrupted at all." Step by step, squeak by squeak on the wooden treads, we walked down the stairs. I chattered away. "It's kind of dark down here, not much light coming through those windows. I sure wish we had some curtains on them because at nighttime, it's creepy. I'll turn on some lights so we can see better."

The basement felt more like a dungeon to me sometimes. That depended on the gatekeeper's mood upstairs. The cement floors were cold. I showed Bruce Dad's little workshop area hidden behind the ton of Mom's stuff. I called it junk. No one would believe it unless they saw it. Bruce didn't say anything about the mess. We headed to the left, entering the rec room part. My Lionel train set was assembled in one corner, a broken sink in the other next to the fireplace we never lit. Across the room, through the double glass doors, was a small bedroom with a single bed next to an old side table with a lamp on it.

I had already told Bruce about my life at home. He knew about Mom's not-so-nice ways behind the Stewart front door. I felt kind of sad as I looked at the bedroom and told Bruce, "This is where my dad sleeps when he is sick or my mom is mad at him." I pointed over to the old gray sagging sofa under the window. Skipping over to it, I plunked down in the middle because of the sag that dips down so far.

"Mom doesn't come down here very often at all, Bruce, so don't worry, this is a private place." Bruce's face brightened, and his tone did too. "So, no one comes down here?"

"Yep. It's just us."

He didn't look at me when he said, "So, those stairs squeak all the time if someone is coming down? Right, Tom?"

"Yep," I said, "I always know if anyone is coming." Bruce made his way over to sit down on the couch where he slid down the slope right into me.

"Hey, Bruce, did you know you are the only one who has ever been allowed in our house, besides our family—and they hardly ever come? My mom must really, really like you."

He just grinned and looked pleased. After that, his face turned a little serious. He pulled himself up by grabbing the arm of the couch. Strolling over to flip off the bright lights, he did a twist where he was at, and then straight back over to me. Without the lights on, there was just enough light so I could still see okay. I wanted to ask him, "Don't we need better light to see my handbook?" Then I thought, *better not say anything, he's my Scout leader.* He sat down next to me again, and put my handbook on the arm of the couch he was trying to keep himself up with. The smell of his Old Spice reminded me of last night. Bruce didn't waste any time before he let me know, "We are going to try this again." I slumped deeper down in the saggy part, and nodded to him just like he was nodding to me. *Is he talking about playing doctor? Oh, yeah. I've still got the same underwear on. Oh, well, they are still clean enough; as of last night.*

"I'm going to massage you again, Tom. You know that this is routine for a Scout leader to do this to a Scout, right?" I nodded again. I didn't know anything different, just that I would do anything to make him happy. He assumed the same position as he had the night before on the floor of the truck. It must have been cold and hard on his knees kneeling on cement. He tilted his head, gesturing me on how I should lay down again. I did exactly what he wanted me to do. I know the drill. Lay low and keep quiet. Especially since Mom was upstairs. *I have to be extra quiet.* I could see what he was doing better than in the truck last night, but I closed my eyes anyway. This time he didn't do any of the massage stuff. He went straight for the unzipping part. I remembered from the night before when he was telling me to, *"Pull 'em up."* Now, it was time for him to "Pull 'em down," for me.

He touched me with the same gentle touch. Was it wrong for me to like it? I was getting the same tickly feelings again. Goosebumps and shivers. His breathing was getting heavier just like before, but so was mine. This time, I was okay with him touching my privates. That is . . . as long as Mother didn't know. She might never let me hang out with him again. *She's so mean sometimes.*

Here it goes, it's straight up again. Kind of funny, just like me standing at attention for Bruce. My eyes are still closed, but the tingling is everywhere; I don't even need to see. He is doing the same motions he did before, but that's okay, it feels good. He always knows exactly what to do.

I hope I do it right this time. Will this be the first skill award badge I get to earn for this? What's happening to me? Oh . . . No wonder he wanted to do this. I hope I don't pee this time. Filling up my lungs with the breath I'm holding, *I think this is a record for me to hold it this long.* Out comes a big, huge sigh . . . I think something else came out too. I feel so strange and shaky. I feel weak, but it felt good. *Thank God, I didn't pee. Am I supposed to thank God for something like that?* I think Bruce is done now. I'm waiting for him to gag . . . but he's not. *Yay! he's not spitting. He's not mad. I did it!* He clears his throat, and I take that as a hint to, "Pull 'em up." He didn't even have to tell me. *Yea me!* I am so happy with myself on how I can obey my Scout leader and do the right thing like he told me to do.

In a low whisper, he said, "You know how it's a secret that you call me Bruce when we are alone, right, Tom? This is a bigger secret, and is even more important that it stays between us, okay? You need to remember that."

I saluted him with, "Yes, Sir, on my honor."

I was zipped and buttoned before Bruce walked over and got the lights turned back on. *I'm getting good at this "pulling 'em up" thing,* I giggle to myself.

The handbook fell to the floor while he was busy with me. Picking it up, he sat down again, teetering on the slant, and opening the book to the first section. Sitting with my hands between my knees, I was curious, so I made sure he was all right. "Bruce, is everything okay?"

He turned toward me, placing his hand on my knee. "Yes, my Prize Scout, it is."

I was smiling so big. *I did it.*

EIGHT

STUCK

BRUCE WAS RELENTLESS. I was eight and naïve. Bruce was eighteen and depraved. Wherever he could get away with getting me alone, he would do it. Whatever he could get away with, he did. He would hype me up by telling me, "You will be earning another skill award this weekend, Tom." Or, "We are going to earn another skill award next weekend, Tom." Beginning at eight . . . and nine . . . then ten years old . . . He continued his routine with me in the same way week after week, month after month, doing the same things to me, in the same way, like that first night in his truck. From the truck to the basement . . . in the truck, in the basement . . . back to the truck.

After two years of it, he said, "I'm getting bored with the same-old, same-old thing. It's time to change things up a bit." I thought he was talking about the places where he took me.

He was cunning. Whether he wanted to fool me or bamboozle any grownup, he was a pro. His portfolio full of creative lies gave him a "no-questions asked" status. Mom may have been over protective in a million ways, but she was clueless to this.

No one suspected anything. No one knew. Especially Bruce's parents. It was happening right underneath their noses—right in their own backyard. The huge, high deck on the back of their house overlooked a yard hidden far down below. The perfect setting for Bruce's intentions.

He put his ulterior motives into motion when he pitched a tent back there. Then he convinced my parents that sleepover after sleepover was all part of the Scout regiment, and necessary to earn some camping or "roughing it" award. After about the seventh sleepover, he came up with another something new.

One day, Bruce walked up to join me in shooting hoops. Our one-on-one dribbling of the ball headed us toward what we called "The Wells." The heavily wooded and secluded area next to my house. I couldn't very well dribble in the woods on the dirt, branches and rocks, so I held my basketball under my arm, and we just walked for a while. Bruce jabbed me with his elbow, "Hey, let's head over to the dense part so no one can find us." Bruce was pretty clever; he had already scoped out the path we were going to take beforehand. Even though I already knew about his secret place. Directing me over to a huge rock that Virgil and I would sometimes jump off from, he pointed, "There's my favorite spot."

I agreed, "Yes, it is. It is where Virgil and I sit when we want to talk."

Bruce sat down on that rock and patted it with his hand, gesturing me to sit down. I wasn't thinking about anything other than being outside in the fresh air talking on what I called *"The Talking Rock"* with Bruce.

"Put the basketball down," he said. "Tom, you know our secret? That secret between me to you?"

I set the basketball down and watched as it rolled and settled in some twigs, trying to ignore the secret he was talking about. He grabbed my shoulder and pulled me back to get my full attention.

"Since you are my Prize Scout, I should be your Prize Scout leader, shouldn't I?"

I didn't know what he meant, but it seemed right to nod my head yes.

"I deserve to feel good too. I mean, it's only fair."

When I realized exactly what he meant, I couldn't get a word out. "Tom, don't you think it's your turn to help me?"

I began to see pictures in my head of what was to come.

"Don't you think you owe me? What I want you to do for me is what I do to you, exactly in the same way."

I knew by then; when Bruce first said that he was giving me a massage, he was not telling the truth. I wished I could have told him off, *Liar, Liar, pants on fire!* I was stupid to ever believe him in the first place.

"Now, Tom, I'm sure you wouldn't want me to tell anyone about what I've done to you, right? You wouldn't want your mom or your dad to know." He paused and looked right at me, "Or even Virgil, right? You will do this for me. With all I've done for you, it's my turn. So be my Prize Scout, and do what I say."

I had never talked back to Bruce, and never planned on it. I had never dared to question him or tell him, "No." So, the inevitable began. He gestured for me to get down on my knees in front of him the same way that he did. Then he looked down at himself where it all started with me. I couldn't get a hold of his zipper with my sweaty fingers; they kept slipping off.

He seemed a little bit impatient, and sounded frustrated, "Come on, Tom, hurry up."

Through my shaking, I got ahold of his baggy pants and boxers and yanked them both down just below his privates. *Oh, my gosh, this creeps me out. What if someone is watching?* Bruce leaned back on his elbows, watching me as if he's making sure I'm going to do it right. "Do it!" He demanded. And then even louder, "Darn it, Tom, Now!"

Coaxing myself, *all I need to do is what he did to me—then I can go.*

I took a deep, deep breath and closed my eyes. *This is sickening.* I was determined to get it over with as fast as I could.

This is so gross. He stinks so bad.

I was choking on my own spit. I stopped and hollered, "I can't do this!" and pulled away from him. Dirt flew up in my eyes. Bruce bolted up. *Oh no, he is mad again.* I fell backwards hitting the ground hard and banging one of my arms on a big branch. It hurt so bad. I felt like the wind was knocked out of me—I couldn't get a sound out. My eyelids were scratching my eyeballs, and stung. I tried rubbing my eyes enough to be able to see. The tears helped.

I could see just enough to see that Bruce was sneering at me. He growled, "Never mind!" Shifting off the rock, he stood up with it all hanging out. "Look at me," he demanded. My eyes were stinging so bad I couldn't. I was frightened by his anger.

This used to be a game . . . it's not fun anymore. Pitching a fit, "Tom, just go . . . get out of here."

Skidding on the dirt to get up, I ran as fast as I could to get away from him. I was too grossed out and freaked out to look back.

Bruce is so pissed off. Is he going to tell someone what has been going on? No doubt that he hates me again. I've always tried to do everything to please him, but I sure didn't this time; I didn't want to. It was just nasty!

I didn't know what to do. I only knew I never wanted to do that again. Thinking about tasting him down there just gave me the heebie-jeebies. It all made me want to hurl up my guts.

I stumbled over the rocks and brush to get out of Bruce's sight. When I stopped to catch my breath, I hunched over to rest my hands on my knees, feeling as if I was going to pass out. *I know . . . I'll head to Virgil's house. I know I can stay there for a while. Bruce won't go there.*

I knocked on Virgil's door, trying to wipe the guilty look off my face. The aroma of dinner hit me when he opened the door. I knew it was rude, but I asked Virgil, "Can I come in for a while?" I really wanted to run to Virgil's mom, cry, and tell her what was going on. But I knew I couldn't. She would tell Mother. It would be so bad if Mother found out. That would be worse than anything I've ever had to do with Bruce.

When Mrs. Hess asked, "Tom, would you like to stay for dinner?", my relief answered, "Yes, ma'am, thank you."

We sat down at the dining room table as a normal family would at dinner time. I wasn't used to all the talking back and forth. It helped settle me down before going home. But I struggled through the entire meal trying to listen to what they were saying. All I could think about was what happened, and the basketball I left behind.

I could have stayed there all night after stuffing myself full of Mrs. Hess' chicken. But it was getting late and I didn't want Mom to get mad and lock the doors on me.

I thanked Mrs. Hess for dinner and made my way home. I looked down the hill towards Bruce's parents' house to see if his truck was gone. Nope, still there. As I went in the front door, the phone was ringing. I don't think Mom heard me come in. On the phone, she said, "Well, hello, Bruce." My gut clenched. *Why is he calling?* "No, Bruce, I'm sorry, Tom is not home yet." She repeated what he was asking, "Oh, so you want Tom to go with you next Tuesday night to earn his swimming skill award? Sure, I don't see why not. Of course, he can."

I was begging in my head, *No, I don't want to go! What excuse can I come up with? Darn it, I don't have any.* Then I remembered what Bruce said, "Now, Tom, I'm sure you wouldn't want me to tell anyone what I've done to you, right? I know you would not want your mom or your dad to know, or even Virgil, right?" I was stuck; I had to go.

Bruce had fooled my parents to the point he really didn't even need to ask for permission anymore. His convincing and conniving manner had snowed my parents like a blizzard. The way he lied to get me alone so far could have won him a customized, dishonest skill award.

For the next five days, I dreaded what was coming. As usual, he picked me up. Bruce took me down to the local swimming pool. I blanked on the actual swimming from that night. All I have is the skill award, reminding me how horrible it was. I would have rather drowned in the pool, rather than do what I had to do to him. In the locker room of all places. He didn't care. He only cared about reaching satisfaction. I remember the sounds of his moans and groans. I hate thinking about it. Mother always told me that the word "hate" is unacceptable. I still hated it. *Why is he doing this to me? Isn't he what they call gay? Is that what they will call me too? There is no way I can tell anyone. I know I am not gay—I like girls.*

I started to dread waking up in the morning. My days turned into more and more days of him making me do what I didn't want to. I thought eventually he would run out of excuses to be with me. I waited and waited for someone . . . anyone . . . to figure him out. But, I just kept on waiting.

When school started the fall before I turned eleven, I was ready to jump up from Cub Scouts to Boy Scouts. One day. Bruce said to me, "Hey, I'll give you a sneak peek at Camp Kilworth." It sparked my interest because it was a camp I hadn't been to yet.

In an upbeat manner, he said, "You can practice and get a head start on earning your archery merit badge. I would be honored to be the first one to take you, Tom. Let's go this weekend. You know your mom will say yes."

I started to get excited . . . but then my heart immediately sank. I gulped and remembered what happened when he was alone with me.

But, I would really love to learn how to shoot with a bow and arrow. *Maybe he won't want to do anything with me this time.* My times with him had become horrible, but I didn't really want to stay at home with my mother either. That was just as horrible in its own way. *I just won't think about the stuff that I don't want to think about.*

Telling him a little white lie, "I can't wait, Bruce."

He gave me an official-sounding order, "Be ready after school on Friday. I will pick you up about five o'clock."

I didn't want to sound stupid and ask what I needed to bring. *I was almost a Boy Scout. I guess I'm supposed to know by now.* I wanted to impress Bruce and follow the motto, "Be prepared" like the perfect Scout I was trying to be. I'd try to "do my best" in everything—even if it involves the gross stuff—just to keep Bruce in a good mood.

If it was a toss-up, I guess I'd have to choose Bruce. At least I got to go somewhere, and it was the only way I could fill up my sash.

NINE

THE WARNING

WITH MY SLEEPING bag, duffle, and pillow stacked by the front door, I waited for Bruce to show up. It was almost time. When I put the yucky stuff out of mind, I was real glad he was in my life. *Not going to think about it, not going to think about it, not going to think about it,* I kept telling myself.

I was excited for him to teach me archery. *Who else would I be able to learn this fun boy stuff from?* Dad was always so busy with work. He didn't have any time left. When Bruce drove up the driveway, right on time, of course, I didn't even give him time to get out of his truck. Grabbing my pile of gear, I yelled out to Mother, "Love you," and out the door I went. Bruce got out of the driver's side, and came to help me with my sleeping bag that was coming unrolled. He grabbed it, telling me, "Tom, I'll put it with your pillow in the back. I have something back there that I don't want you to touch or go near."

He didn't offer to tell me what it was, so I didn't ask. To challenge my authority was not a good idea . . . ever. So, I walked around to the side of the truck and handed him my duffle. Far enough away from the back so he didn't have to remind me again. Bruce assured me, "I will put it on top of everything else. Also, Tom, I didn't roll your sleeping bag back up—there is no reason to, we will just put it straight in the tent after we pitch it up. We don't have to be so Scout official when it's

75

just us, right?" I took my Prize Scout position in the passenger seat and buckled up. Lickety split, I locked the door before Bruce even had to tell me. From what I heard, the camp was not too far away. We drove through some neighborhoods nearby, and then kept going. I was getting lost in my head and hesitantly asked, "Where are we?" No answer. He just kept driving.

Finally, at the end of a side road, we arrived at a fenced-off entrance with a big, worn wooden sign overhead, carved out with letters saying Camp Kilworth. Tall tree trunks with the bark shaved off, bound together with rope, looked like an opening to a secret place on the other side.

We drove ahead on a gravel road and stopped in front of the driveway of what had to be the ranger's cabin.

The door opened when a big, tall woman ranger with a long gray braid, came stomping out in big black boots. She was kind of bully looking. I didn't know a lady could be a ranger; she looked more like a man.

Bruce looked down on me as if to say, "Just stay quiet." I was already good at the "lay low and keep quiet" thing. He seemed happy that it was a woman ranger. He said to me, "I'm sure she will let us stay even without our troop."

He rolled down his window as she got closer. She said a not so-friendly "Hello." Until she recognized Bruce, then her mood seemed to improve with him trying to convince her, "I am bringing our newest star Boy Scout here to advance him a little bit on some skills. He needs to earn his archery merit badge. I brought my tent, ma'am, and . . . is it okay with you if we find a spot to stay the night?"

"Okay. Just keep your surroundings clean," she reminded us. That response from her was enough to make Bruce's face brighten up. He looked like he just earned a merit badge for himself. He thanked her twice and we drove on.

Huge trees lined the twists and turns alongside a river that ran through a deep crevasse. Bruce took his foot off the gas pedal long enough to point out the archery range on the left.

I showed a big excited smile, and chanted, "Yeah, yeah, yeah."

"First, we are going to find a place to pitch the tent before it gets dark. We won't have time tonight to shoot any arrows, I'm sorry about that, Tom. We will try our hand at that tomorrow." He put the truck in reverse, and snaked back up to a Y in the road. Gradually, it became more narrow, and looked more like a trail—as it went deeper into the woods. "Don't worry, I have four-wheel drive. This will be fun."

He revved the truck as he went up the hill on the winding path, so he wouldn't get stuck. Branches were scraping the windows. "It's getting bumpier up here," I said, laughing, as I bounced in my seat. *Nothing's gonna stop us cool Scouts in Bruce's cool Scout from making it.*

Bruce stopped, "This is the perfect site. Let's get to unpacking, my Prize Scout. We'll set up over there in the clearing."

We both got out of the truck at the same time. I stepped back to watch Bruce open the back. He moved my stuff out of the way to get his two-man tent. Underneath, there was his cooler and lantern. I never had to worry about him forgetting anything. He was always prepared, just like the Scout Motto.

Do I offer to help him? Bruce didn't know he was answering me when he told me what was back there, "I had to bring my gun since we are out in the middle of nowhere. That's why I told you earlier not to go near there." Then he tucked the gun in the back of his pants, hidden under his shirt.

We set up the tent on a cushion of some fallen leaves. It didn't take long at all—we had practiced setting it up so many times in his backyard. We didn't have an air mattress though. "No air mattress needed out here," Bruce said. "We are going to rough it a bit."

"Tom, go ahead and drag the cooler over there and I will start a fire."

When I grabbed the handle, it felt really full. I opened it up. *Bruce is so cool.* There was junk food galore and everything I didn't get at home. *Awesome, I see some hot dogs too.*

"Hey, Bruce, do we need branches for the hot dogs and marshmallows you packed in here?"

"Yes, please. I want to make sure we have enough so we don't have to scrounge after dark." *He's smart.* I was feeling smart too as I had already thought of that.

He shot a thumbs-up my way. I felt so cool and responsible. But when he said, "Oh no, I forgot matches and my lighter," I was surprised. He never forgets anything. He didn't seem upset. He said, "I know what, we can light a fire the Scout way. But first, Tom, we need to get our stuff in the tent."

He handed me our pillows, and he took the sleeping bags in his arms. Since mine was already unrolled, it was dragging on the ground. His eyes lured me over to help him in the tent.

"I'll get the lantern," I said.

"Nah, we don't need it yet." Kneeling down right behind him, I helped Bruce by shoving in the rest of the trailing sleeping bag while I crawled in on my knees. He zipped down the opening to close it up on us.

We shuffled around to get the sleeping bags and pillows arranged just right. Bruce looked at me, and then down at himself.

Then . . . I knew.

He patted his hand on his knee for me to come over and sit next to him, just like he had patted the rock at The Wells.

Bruce looked anxious. Instead of waiting for me to scoot over to sit next to him, he just barked, "Take your clothes off." Before I could even think, Bruce lay down and ripped his clothes off and kicked them to the corner of the tent.

I tried not to look directly at him. I was fiddling with my clothes, making it look like I was doing what he expected. I could still see him looking at me out of the corner of my eye.

"Hurry up, you slowpoke." I thought, *I have to do what he says.* Then my mouth opened up like an idiot. "Bruce, do we really have to do this again?"

He sat back up bare naked, and hovered over me.

I remembered how scared he had made me before. "Tom, you are to do what you are told. Remember the gun? The one I had in the back of my pants?" His angry words convinced me that he really meant it. "Do you see where the gun is now? I'm not kidding." I looked over where he put it down in the corner of the tent.

Choked up and hardly able to swallow, I put my face in my hands and squeaked out, "Please forgive me, Bruce. I'm sorry."

"You know, Tom, I don't do all I do for you to get nothing in return. Just remember that! I will never help you or take you anywhere again if you do not reciprocate. Do I have to remind you again of who I could tell?"

When I finally got my clothes all the way off, I shoved them in the opposite corner of his. It was getting dark out and the cold made me start to shiver. Except for the shivering, I was still as could be, waiting for him to tell me what to do.

Bruce's bad mood turned to better when he shared what was going to happen in that tent, "We are going to take turns tonight. You got that?"

My "Yes, Sir," kept him calm. The word "gun" kept repeating in my ears. It all meant that I was to obey him.

His clammy hands latched on to my shoulders, and forced me back until my head hit the pillow. *I guess it's me first.* With my eyes shut, I concentrated on squeezing them tighter so I could shift to thinking about something else—like the rock under my back that hurt like heck.

I was starting to figure him out. He always started out as the nice guy. All those promises. But just like that, he changes into somebody else. I wanted to be somebody else too.

He was grunting. He then stopped and looked up at me, "Get some life in you, kid! You are boring!" His insult sprung up a brilliant idea in me. I'm going to fake that I like it. *Does he want me to make noises like he does? Alrighty, then. If that's what he wants—that's what he gets. Here goes . . .* "Yep, you got it going on, now." He reassured me, "Yeah, Tom, that's it!" In survival mode, I told myself, *I will do whatever it takes to get through this.* It was getting so dark in the tent, I couldn't see him very well. At least he couldn't see my fooling face. I gave him what I hoped sounded like a satisfied sigh, and a great big "ahhh" to reassure him he did a good job. And then came the moment I truly dreaded. *I'm not really doing this, I'm not really doing this,* I pretended. Then his gun came to mind. He lay himself down and warned me about the gun. "I don't want to have to reach over and place it on your naked skin so you can feel how serious I am."

I hope he saw my head shake like my "Yes, Sir," because I sure couldn't get the words out.

My jaw was locking. All I could hope for was for him to hurry up. It took forever . . . but then, finally!

I'm glad he couldn't see the rolling going on with my eyes.

It was pitch dark. I was freezing naked while Bruce had fallen asleep and started to snore. Naked is not what I wanted to be. He may want to do it all over again. I didn't want to reach for my clothes—there was no way I wanted to wake him.

Slowly feeling around for the opening of the sleeping bag, I was glad it was already unzipped so I wouldn't make that noise. Easing myself inside in slow motion, I did my usual lay low and keep quiet.

Bruce was still snoring away in the dark. Outside the frogs and crickets were making their night sounds. I was so hungry. I didn't even get to eat any hot dogs. Bruce's snoring was helping me remember the normal Bruce again. Most of the time, I felt safe with him—not when we were doing the gross stuff together—but other times. At least it was over for the night, so I could forget it ever happened. I can get to sleep that way.

My tired mind took only a few minutes to pass out, but then it felt like only a few minutes to wake back up screaming.

Bruce quickly sat up and grabbed me. "Are you okay, are you okay?"

"I was so scared Bruce. Was I dreaming?"

"You must have been, Tom," he said to calm me down. "I must have dozed off too. What were you dreaming about anyway?" "I usually can't remember a lot about my dreams, but that was a bad one that I could. It was Bruce pointing his gun at me. We were still naked in the nightmare too. I couldn't tell Bruce about it. It really might make him mad; instead, I ended up telling him, "I can't remember, Sir, but it really scared me."

Bruce whispered, "Go back to sleep," as he rubbed my back. It lulled me back to sleep again. Like a mommy's touch I never had.

The birds chirping at sunrise woke me. It took me a bit to get a grip on where I was. I had no idea what time it was, but I doubted I could go back to sleep again. I was still shaken up about my nightmare. It felt good to know Bruce was there to protect me. I was trembling, it was so cold. This roughing it bit is not for this Scout. The stupid rock was still under me. I scuffled around in my sleeping bag to try and keep warm—that's when Bruce woke up. With his eyes opening, his groggy voice asked if I was okay. He was kind of rude with his comment, "I hope so—no wussy Scouts here, you know?"

I guessed he meant a coward. Gosh, no way would I want to be that.

"It's cold out here, ain't it, Tom? I can see my breath."

I was glad Bruce was the first to say how cold it was. I didn't want to be the "wussy Scout" he talked about.

With my teeth chattering, I got a few words out, "Yes, I'm freezing!" Right after I said that, I knew I should have just kept my mouth frozen shut. Bruce slid out of his sleeping bag and slid down in mine. My thoughts raced, *Uh, we are both naked and our bodies are touching from naked head to naked toe . . . he must be gay.* I was tempted to say those words to Bruce, but I wasn't that dumb. He tried to bluff me. "I just want to keep my Prize Scout warm.

I said, "uh huh," to go along with it. In one minute, I was scared of Bruce. Then in another, I felt safe with him. At other times, he just plain-old grossed me out.

"You do remember about my gun . . . right, Tom?"

"Yes, Sir."

"So, you are not going to tell anyone about this weekend either . . . right?"

"No, Sir."

I can't even tell anyone about my nightmare either because it would be tattling on Bruce. If he found out I had opened my mouth, he might get so mad that he may actually make my nightmare come true. This must stay just between my Scout leader and me, his Prize Scout.

He was starting to make his move. Rubbing his disgusting, hairy body up against mine. Bruce must have thought he was being clever and tricking me. "I'm just trying to get your circulation moving." I took on my shut-up mode until he was done. He snuck his arm around me—I guess groping my privates was what he was after. He chuckled, "We have to keep them warm too, you know."

I was just waiting for him to stop. I couldn't help it, I blurted, "I really have to pee." He said he did too. Good thing too, if he wanted to get gross again, I might have peed all over him again. *Maybe I should have?* Maybe that would make him stop. He threw my clothes to me, and said, "Well, I guess it's time to finally make that fire." He left the tent, and it left me thinking, *He's not hurting me, I guess it's not that bad. Really, it's not. Maybe it's worth it just being with him.*

Hollering from the driver's door of his truck, "Guess what? I found my lighter! Woo-hoo! How about we make those hot dogs you wanted last night for breakfast, my Prize Scout?"

Hot dogs for breakfast? I cracked a smile and happily said, "Sure, yes, Sir!" *Bruce is so good to me.*

TEN

THE THREAT IS REAL

AFTER OUR HOT dog breakfast, we packed the truck and cleaned the campsite like the ranger lady told us to. I didn't realize we were going to leave so early, but Bruce did keep his promise and introduced me to the archery range before we left. I felt so clumsy—I couldn't seem to hit the target even once. Bruce would not be calling me his prize archer any time soon. As we drove out on the gravel road of Camp Kilworth, Bruce said, "You did okay, Tom. Practice makes perfect." That was the first time I ever heard "okay" was good enough. I wasn't sure how to take that, yet coming from Bruce, it felt great.

"You do have a major head start on the other boys, even if you didn't get much practice time in." Then with a sideways glance at me, he suggested, "I think we should probably come back one more time, just the two of us again to give you more practice. I want you to master the art of archery so you have the right to wear the badge. Wouldn't it be great if you could get yours before any of the others, and show it off in front of them?"

"For sure, Sir!" Then pondering what he said, he told me that I did "okay." *I wonder if he meant the bow and arrow stuff, or if he meant the gross stuff in the tent?* Bruce always had a way of making me feel good about myself.

"Hey, Tom," he said, "If there was ever was a Prize Scout merit badge, you'd be the first one to get it from me."

Driving home, Bruce surprised me when he said, "I'm going to be moving out of my parents' house soon."

"What? Why?" Anyone might think I would have been glad. But I was sad.

Bruce saw it on my face. He tried to make me feel better, "No worries, Tom, I will still be over a lot to mooch dinner off my mom."

Before I knew it, we were pulling into my driveway. I was still zoning out on the thought of him moving. *Wait a minute, I wonder if that means our secret will be over?* I felt torn between being glad and sad.

While putting the truck in park, Bruce stressed, "Now remember, Tom, our secret is our secret, and it's going to stay our secret. When I move out, it will continue to be our secret—it always will be."

Well, I guess that answers my question. That part is not over.

We both got out and shut our doors at the same time. I waited for Bruce to open the back of the Scout to hand me my stuff. I didn't want to risk disobeying his rules again. Besides, guns scare the bejeebers out of me.

Bruce could see I was upset. Trying to cheer me up, he shoved my tightly rolled sleeping bag over my right hand like one of those big sock-'em bop-'em boxing gloves and punched it. I put my neck down toward him to hang the duffle strap around it, and shoved my pillow under my left arm. All I said to him was a distant, "Thanks."

Bruce tried one more time, "I'm sure your mom would let you come and stay the night with me wherever I move to. Don't you think so?"

Without turning around, I shrugged my shoulders, and said a quiet, "Thanks again," and walked slowly to the house.

He called out to me before I got to the front door. "Hey, Tom." I stopped and turned around to what he said. "When our Boy Scout troop starts up, we will be heading to Camp Hahobas the first part of October. There is a cool gun range there. You'll probably do well at shooting a gun." I know for sure I will have to keep shooting a secret from Mother. There is no way she'd let me go. I may suck at archery, but I am a prize secret keeper.

"That sounds neat, Bruce. I can't wait." My mind had shifted away from him moving. *Maybe I won't be so afraid of guns if he teaches me to shoot. Bruce is good in that way.*

I gave him a fast wave goodbye.

Our family finished off that summer with another camping trip, one last hoorah, right before my eleventh birthday. The trailer experiences I had growing up with were not getting any better. My parents pulled the twenty foot Shasta trailer behind our Chitty Chitty Bang Bang Suburban, and we'd set off for our camping adventure down the 0.8-mile stretch—just one minute away from our house at the State Park. The same park with the bathroom that my dad considered his own. Such an odd family, us Stewarts. Dad drove around and around until he found the perfect campsite. And around and around again. It was like walking around a Christmas tree lot, searching forever for the perfect tree. Thirty minutes later, and after Mom and Dad's thirty minutes of arguing, they'd settle on one.

We could have stayed home if all they were going to do was argue. Situating our parking spot to set up camp at our so-called happy home away from home would have been better to either skip it, or go somewhere out in the middle of nowhere so no one had to listen to them.

Camping trips are supposed to be a good bonding time for a family. Not for the Stewarts. So many times, I either just wanted to get lost, run away, or even be kidnapped for that matter. Anything would have been better.

No wonder why Bruce was my escape.

My world exploded when we came home that Sunday from camping, and we found his note taped to the door, telling us he had moved out over the weekend. I dropped whatever I was holding and it all fell to the ground. Of course, Mom yelled at me to pick it up, but her words didn't faze me. I felt alone without my Scout leader.

I was so mixed up. *Why am I so sad?* Glad crossed my mind for a split second because of the gross stuff, but didn't last because I missed him a whole bunch more. *Am I crazy for missing him?*

The only thing that made me feel better was that I remembered I was going to Boy Scout camp that next weekend with him at Camp Hahobas. If my parents decided on the spur of the moment for one last camping hoorah, Boy Scouts and Bruce would get me out of it, for sure.

Then I remembered that Bruce had said, "I'm sure your mom would let you come and stay the night with me wherever I move to." I stuck to that plan.

If there was ever a time I needed to get out of something, all I had to do was beg Bruce to take me to his house instead. Bruce was teaching me how to good at being sneaky.

October came quick. When I hopped in Bruce's truck to go to Camp Hahobas, the first thing he said was, "When we get there, remember not to mention the gun or the gun range to anyone else at the camp. I'm only going to take you and only you. It has to stay a hush hush thing, okay?"

I felt special. "Yes, Sir." I loved being the Scout leader's chosen pet. Once we got there, I kept nudging him and asking him when we could go to the gun range. He gave me his dominant look of "cool it." I shrank down knowing I had messed up. No roughing it this time on the hard ground—we had cabins with bunks and mattresses.

After dinner time at the mess hall, the boys were all settling down by the campfire. Bruce glanced over at me. His eyebrows questioned me. "Ready?" He walked away from the fire and headed for the cabin. I waited a few minutes, stood up, and snuck off the same way. None of the kids even paid attention. They were all laughing, telling stories, and whittling away on their roasting sticks for marshmallows. I spotted Bruce's shadow, and met up with him to hike towards the gun range. Once we were out of sight, Bruce turned on his flashlight to lead the way. The gun range was quite a hike. *I hope nobody wonders where we went and comes to find us,* I thought. I wanted to shoot Bruce's gun bad.

Stomping through the path, Bruce shone his light on the gun range. "May I, may I, please, Bruce?"

He gruffly changed the depth in his answer, "Just stop, Tom. You need to stop. Just settle down."

"Sorry, Bruce. I will." I followed him over to a humongous tree. He turned around and leaned his body up against the heavily barked trunk.

It must have hurt his backside when he slid down the side and landed hard on the ground. I didn't want him to hear me laugh at him when he dropped the flashlight on his way down. It fell away, and dimmed to off. It was definitely quite creepy with how dark it was. Bruce's hand grabbed my arm and pulled me down to where he had landed. I knew exactly what that meant. I shook my head sideways. Not that he could see me, but I knew I couldn't say no out loud.

He voiced a deep harsh "We are not here to shoot guns. We are here to do what we do best to each other!"

The dark sound of his words scared me.

I couldn't speak. As usual, he didn't seem to care how I felt.

This was exactly how my nightmare played out. Now, it was coming to life.

He was kind of rough this time, yanking me into place right where he wanted me to be. I didn't realize that his pants were down past his knees already. Bruce rustled for the flashlight and turned it on—shining right at me like I was the star on stage. Acting like an emcee, he used the flashlight as a microphone and announced, "Here is our good Scout Tom, and he is going to obey the Scout Motto by 'doing his best.'" As he aimed the flashlight back on me, I forced myself to fake a laugh at his stupid joke. My eyes were blinded by the light, but at least I didn't have to see him. Earplugs would have been perfect so I wouldn't have had to listen to him either.

At least he was quick. "You know my Prize Scout, if they had a merit badge for what you just did, you would have earned it."

Then, "What's that?" he said before I heard him pull his pants up faster than he could shush me.

Someone was calling our names in the distance. "Oh, darn it, they are looking for us. Stand up, Tom, and wipe your mouth off."

My heart was banging like a drummer on a drum set. Bruce yelled back, "Yeah, we are over here. We were just heading back."

It was our other leader with a few Scouts behind him. "Just making sure you weren't lost."

Bruce was quick in his response. "I'm showing Tom how to rifle through the dark to find the rifle range and shotgun range . . . get it? Rifle." He laughed out loud at his own joke as he was trying to make it believable. Then Bruce riled up the boys by suggesting a game he said he heard of called '*Scout Seek Out.*' "Then we all can try and find the gun range together in the dark, just like Tom here."

Dishonesty just comes natural for Bruce. He had become an expert. I just kept my mouth shut. I was an expert at that. Bruce woke me up bright and early the next morning before anyone else was up. Without saying a word, he ordered me by a swift motion with his head to get up and go with him. He walked quietly towards the door to wait for me to get my clothes on. *I hope he's finally taking me to the gun range this morning.* Out the door, trying not to make a sound. Off we went; trekking on the trail, taking a hard right through the woods. *Feels like the same way we went last night.*

Bruce wasn't saying much. I glanced up at him, and he said, "I'm taking you on a short walk to show you the abandoned sleeping hall. I just thought it would be cool for just the two of us. They call it, 'Fruitcake Lodge.'" I covered my mouth and bent way over so he wouldn't see me holding back my laugh. He might get mad because there was no way I could tell him why I was cracking up. I'm glad he was walking in front of me and not paying attention. It wasn't just the name that was so funny, it was how I'd heard people say that men who like boys are called fruitcakes. *Bruce must really be a fruitcake.* We were heading to the right place for him to visit . . . Fruitcake Lodge.

The door was cracked open and we stepped in. It was old and dusty, with cobwebs hanging all over the place. *It must be haunted.* "This place creeps me out," slipped out of my mouth.

Maybe he thought he could make me feel better by saying, "Don't worry, I brought my gun."

That for sure was not going to make me feel better. His gun to me didn't feel like protection—it was threatening. I clung on to Bruce's arm. Then, I remembered the wussy words he used, so I let go and told myself, *Be brave.* I followed around behind him as he was making sure the place was completely empty.

"Yup, we're good," were the words he used to try and make me feel better. Bruce led me into a corner where I waited for him to tell me what we were doing there. He didn't need to tell me. After Bruce's gun threat was imprinted on my brain, I was too afraid to do anything but to wait on what he wanted.

Bruce was stern. "No one else is going to interrupt my time with my Prize Scout again. I am going to finish what we started last night." I pulled down my pants as he gestured for me to do. His notion for me to sit down on the floor had my butt cold already. I just let him do his thing. Pretending to like it, I was thankful when he was done. Surprisingly, he didn't ask for anything in return. I brushed off my backside and pulled 'em up. I started some small talk to cover up how I really felt.

Bruce was already standing when he instructed me, "We had better get back before they know we are gone. We can go to the mess hall and ask if we can help with breakfast. I'm sure someone is awake there. Then we don't need to explain why we were gone to the others."

Another one of his nifty cover-ups. I followed him out the door like I followed him in—like a puppy dog trained to heel. Mother taught this perfectly obedient pet well.

ELEVEN

PRETTY RISKY

EVER SINCE HE threatened me with his gun, the rest of what he already hadn't taken from me went missing. I never questioned him if he was kidding . . . I knew he wasn't.

His two quick, one long rings of the doorbell shut me down into his prize robot—already programmed by my, "Yes, Sir."

Eventually, my life spun in circles like a merry-go-round—dizzy . . . sick to my stomach . . . or wanting to jump off; slowing long enough to see where Bruce's Russian Roulette would take me for him to get his rocks off next.

My body was changing. Pubic hair was starting to grow on me down there. Under my armpits too. There was a new squeak in my voice that sounded so girlie. I wasn't liking it at all.

Bruce joked with me about it all the time. "I think your little pal and his buddies are getting bigger down there, Tom. Ha, ha. It's about time. I'm waiting to show you more pleasure. And, then, vice versa—if you know what I mean?"

I didn't know what he had meant by more pleasure. *What else could he possibly do to me that he hadn't already done? I don't have any girl parts. He must be thinking about taking me to his apartment.*

When I heard that Boy Scout Troop 310 was folding for the upcoming year, I was very disappointed. Just one year into it. Not enough boys, not enough leadership, except for Bruce. He said he was more than willing to juggle all the boys himself. However, one person wasn't enough to carry the troop alone. So, that was a no-go for him. Bruce was even more disappointed than I was.

When I thought about Bruce and the other Scouts, I got a strange feeling in my stomach. It really did bug me. I wondered if he had played with other boys the way he had played with me. I wanted to be his only Prize Scout. I don't want him to have any others. In some ways, I was glad the troop was folding. The secret stuff grossed me out, but for me to be Scout leader's pet was all I thought about.

Hold on, Bruce is still part of another troop. If I'm not in a troop with him anymore, he might just find another Prize Scout from that one to replace me. Bruce read the puzzled look all over my face. "Tom, we will never stop hanging out as buddies—Scout or not—you got that?" I nodded my head up and down, like really fast. His words helped. But I kind of wondered what kind of excuse he was going to give my mom now that Scouting events couldn't be used. I was sure he would be as clever as he has always been with whatever it was.

Mom would have made me quit Scouts in the upcoming year regardless. She went back to when she warned me in the first place. "It has taken up way too much of your time. I told you that you could join, as long as it didn't interfere with school, sports, church, or my viola. And, it has. Sunday school needs you to help out."

I had missed being at church, especially after being chosen first out of everyone by the Sunday school teacher to help her teach. I felt so important, smart, and; most of all, appreciated by her. It also just might have had something to do with the crush I had on her. That happened a lot with my women teachers. Being the Sunday school teacher's pet also meant getting to take all the leftover snacks home with me.

I was also slacking on my viola lessons. I know for sure it hadn't hurt my schoolwork. I made sure of that. I didn't want to face the ultimate wrath of Mother if it ever did.

However, she did have a point with my viola. I was pretty good at playing, but there was always room to get better—I got that mindset from Mother. I really liked my viola teacher, whom I just happened to have a huge crush on also.

Mother had another harebrained idea and signed me up to try out for the Youth Symphony. I'm sure she dreamed about sitting in the front row, dressed in her glitz and glamour, boasting about her son sitting in first chair.

My additional lessons would be a lot of hard work to get there, but spending as much time as possible with my music teacher is what I was thinking about.

On the flip side of Mother's expectations, her pride had to swallow that I almost didn't make it. It didn't matter to me. All that time I got to spend with my viola teacher earned me the title of music teacher's pet, just as I'd hoped for.

I clenched onto whatever personal feelings that belonged to me, trying to keep Mother's invasion out of my life. She couldn't consume my mind if I didn't let her. The part of my life where Mom showed me off in public didn't feel as if it was much of a benefit to me. If there was any praise at all, she'd soak it right up out from underneath me. Scouts had been the only reprieve from her pride. I was looking forward to being able to join up with Scouts eventually, but for right then, I would focus on the new year school starting, becoming a teenager, and playing as many sports as possible so I could keep a hold of me, myself, and I.

The day Bruce drove up in his Scout, towing a trailer with a big boat on it, I ran outside; just as excited as he was. "That is so cool, Bruce."

"Tom, you are the first person I wanted to show. I told you I would still be here for you." Anxious to ask me, "So, Tom, I'm sure you would want to go out on my maiden voyage with me and be my deckhand, right?"

I was antsy, hoping he would ask me—and he did! *I am the luckiest kid ever.*

Standing next to Bruce, I noticed I was finally as tall as him. Seemingly I had sprouted up tall just like that. Looking eye to eye, I thanked him for being in my life—Scouts or no Scouts. He friend-punched me in the arm and said, "No matter what, Tom—no matter what!"

We both turned around when we heard the front door slam and saw my dad moseying out towards us. He complimented Bruce. "Wow, very nice."

Bruce proudly replied, "Thanks, Mr. Stewart. Is it okay if Tom goes out on the first cruise with me on Commencement Bay this evening?"

With a deep chuckle, Dad didn't hesitate to say, "I would really like to join you." My dad was good at inviting himself places.

Bruce wasn't expecting that. He cleared his throat when he looked at me, and said, "Sure. Yes, of course, Mr. Stewart."

That was the biggest white lie I had ever heard.

I knew Bruce wanted it to be just him and me, and I kind of wanted that too. But he couldn't really say no to Dad, even though he wanted to. Unfortunately, I had become closer to Bruce than my own actual father. It was sad for me, but it was the truth. All I could think about was getting on that boat and zooming around the water. How cool it was going to be. One good thing about Dad coming with us, Bruce wouldn't risk doing any of his gross stuff with me.

Boy, was I wrong.

We backed the boat off the trailer into the water and waited for Bruce to park the Scout. He ran toward the dock, and jumped in the boat like a true captain would. I thought, *I know what I am today. I am Captain's Pet. Yah!*

Bruce climbed up the ladder on the flying bridge, and turned the key. The sound of the motor was loud. The propeller roughed up the standing water, stirring up the boats surrounding us. He gave us a thumbs-up, pointed for us both to sit down, and we were off. He had to go slow through the marina. Wanting to sound like a true seaman, Dad mentioned, "Tom, the waves we're making are called a wake." Bruce's boat was rocking back and forth, making me kind of seasick. *Not going to puke; not going to puke,* trying to psyche myself out. Swerving around the boats anchored here and there, Bruce headed to the middle of the bay and idled it out and away from any of the other boats. "Skipper Stewart, would you like to take over?"

At first, I thought he was talking to me. *Uh, no.* He was talking to my dad. Dad practically jumped up out of his seat and rushed up the ladder to take over the steering wheel.

"Have you done this before, Skipper Stewart?" I wasn't even sure if my dad had ever driven a boat before. I'm not sure he would have told the truth if he hadn't.

"Well, as a matter of fact, Captain Bruce, Sir, I have." Dad pulled down the big lever causing the boat to speed up. Bruce patted him on his back and told him, "I think you can handle this from here. I will be down below deck to the head. I gotta go—like bad."

Blurting out, "What's a head?", Bruce told me it is the bathroom. Dad joined in, "And the kitchen is called the galley." I was a little confused as to why they weren't just called the kitchen and the bathroom. But sitting in the back of the boat with the wind in my face made me happier than I had been in a while, and that's all I cared about.

Bruce began climbing down the rungs of the ladder. He then grabbed his hat off his head and waved it in the air with an, "Ahoy, mateys." At the bottom, he dipped down low enough below the deck so my dad couldn't see him from the flying bridge. He gave me his superior officer in-charge look—the look I dreaded.

Panning between the both of them . . . when my dad wasn't looking, I scrunched my lips together and opened my eyes really wide, mouthing to Bruce, "No! My dad is here." He also scrunched his lips together back to me, and opened his eyes even wider. With one hand still holding on to a rung of the ladder, his other hand pulled up to mimic a gun pointed at me.

I exhaled, knowing I had better get up. Before I did, my dad looked back down at me from the bridge. He was having fun and wore a huge smile. I had been having fun too until Bruce put a kink in that one. I could only shout to my dad to make sure he heard me, "I'm going down below to lie down. My tummy is upset." I wanted to yell to him for help . . . but the fear of his gun inside my head was yelling louder. I grabbed on to the side of the boat. Hand over hand, I got over to the doorway, walked through, and down two steps into the cabin below deck. There he was. Sitting on the bed straight ahead—waiting for me. The bed was shaped like a triangle. It went way underneath to the front pointy part of the boat. I didn't know what that part of the boat is called. *Bad time to ask.*

I lifted my eyebrows to him, pointing up with my finger to my dad right above us. Bruce had that hard, stern look back on his face, telling me to "Shut up."

I moved over toward him before he had to tell me. I knew I had better before he got mad. I crawled on the bed and squeezed in the tight quarters next to him. Bruce said nothing to me the entire time. There was too much noise from the boat to hear even if he did. And that made it impossible for my dad to hear what was going on.

Bruce took charge over me. *I have never seen him like this.* He jerked my pants down and my underwear came down with them. He did the same to his. He eased over me and crushed me under him. I couldn't move. At that moment, it felt as if we were buried in a coffin together. I would have rather been dead for real. He twisted his body around so that his testicles were in my face and mine were in his. I had a random thought about how Mom would have a heart attack if she heard me call my privates testicles.

Out of the corner of my eye, there it was—his gun—sitting on the counter right next to us.

What if Dad stops the boat and comes down? That scared me more than being scared for myself. *Would Bruce really hurt my dad?*

I'll wait until he does what he's going to do to me; then I will know what he wants me to do to him. In my awkward position, I was curious as to what he was doing. He's never done that to those before. It kind of hurt and kind of didn't. Bruce hit his head on the top, but he was too busy doing what he was doing to care.

Should I do the same thing to him? Okay, here goes. Ugh, if I don't puke from the swaying of the boat, it would probably be from this. Yuck, hairs were in my mouth and my face felt smothered by his two squishy water balloons.

Suddenly, we heard the boat motor groan to slow down. Bruce tugged on the mattress and rolled himself off me, frantically grabbing his clothes. Oh good, I can breathe. I "pulled 'em up" as fast as I could. Bruce rushed out the door, making sure my dad wasn't on his way down. I saw his feet climbing two rungs up the ladder, "Everything okay, Skipper Stewart? Sorry I took so long, it must have been something I ate. I wouldn't go down there if I were you; the smell is overwhelming. I'm surprised Tom is still napping with the stink I left behind. He must be feeling even more seasick than he thought."

In a make-believe pirate voice, Dad answers him, "Aye, aye, Captain, everything is great. Where would you like me to go next? I know—since you are the captain, and I am the skipper, maybe Tom can be the navigator."

Bruce leaned down to call me through the door, "All hands on deck." His hand gestures me to come out. So, I obeyed my orders, and climbed out to hear Bruce say, "As captain of this vessel, I proclaim our crew is complete."

I climb up the ladder to the bridge saying, "Ahoy, mateys." Bruce chuckled in his own pirate voice, "You, Tom, have been chosen as the honorary, prize navigator of my ship. And it's your job to tell the skipper which way he needs to go."

In my own made-up pirate voice, I said, "I will take a stab at navigating this vessel and see if it will lead us to some hidden treasure."

It was fun that they were both playing my pirate game with me. With one of my eyes squinted shut like it was covered with a pirate patch, "Hey-oh, Captain Bruce, us mateys would like to know the name you dubbed this ship?"

Bruce pumped up his chest and said, "Yo ho! Aye lad, I was waiting for you to ask . . . 'Prize Scout' be the name." Then he winked at me. I made sure my dad was not looking at me—my wink and crooked smile back at him said it all. For my dad's sake, I shouted with my fist, raised to mimic a salute to the ship, "Well, shiver me timbers, Captain."

Dad placed my hands on the wheel, and showed me what to do. I increased the speed with the lever like Dad did and the boat started to go faster. *Oh, crap, I don't like this.* I felt uneasy and off balance. After a bit, the rocking of the boat back and forth bothered me so much that I handed the wheel right back to Dad. I couldn't tell either one of them I was scared. Instead, "I'm still not feeling well. I feel like I need to hurl." I took a seat up there next to Dad, where he was back in the driver's seat. I crossed my arms and felt ashamed for not being better at that. Bruce is probably thinking that I'm a "wussy" again. *I guess I really suck as a shipmate—no prize navigator here.* Sitting there, listening to the crashing waves gave me plenty of time to wallow in feeling sorry for myself.

I glanced around behind me, down to the lower deck to see if Bruce was there. He was sitting on the seat at the back of the boat with his body twisted around; his head resting on his hand, staring off into the water behind us. *I hope he's not sad.* Maybe just disappointed he didn't get to finish. I was relieved it was quick. But I never liked letting him down. He does so much for me and he makes me happy. *I want to do the same for him.*

I wasn't quite sure what I was feeling. Any feelings I used to have were now buried in my fear of his gun.

I don't need to think about it right now. At least it's over for today.

TWELVE

NOT THE ONLY ONE

AT MEEKER JUNIOR High, I engulfed myself in all the sports available. The longer I was at school, the less time I'd have to be at home. Flag football, soccer, baseball, and obviously, basketball. I loved basketball. I was told I was a "shoo-in" and a "natural." Since the year before, I had grown to six feet. I could be kind of clumsy in other stuff, but with sports, I was focused and determined. A Stewart plays to win.

Competitive should have been my middle name. I don't know if it was sports that brought that out in me, or just my last name. Needless to say, my pride inflated with each win, and even greater when the pictures were published in the local newspaper with 'The most valuable, star athlete' caption underneath.

Slam dunks were my specialty—stealing the ball, and jump shots too. I had all the moves. All those street basketball scrambles must have done the trick.

All the flirty looks from the cheerleaders helped me play better—but I had to focus to keep my eyes on the ball and not their cute little skirts and waving pompoms.

If Bruce showed up for my games, my goal was to show off in front of him so he could be even more proud of his prize athlete.

The nights that Mom and Dad weren't there, Bruce was in seventh heaven. He had me all to himself. That's when his apartment became a part of his finagling. His crafty art of asking my mom if I could stay the night with him. Even on a school night, she'd let me go. That blew me away. When it came to Bruce, she never said no . . . ever. When the abuse was at the front of my mind, the excuses I tried to come up with to get out of going, Bruce overruled them. Finally, I just quit trying. For me, it was still a toss-up. Bruce and me alone? Or, Mom barking away at me? It didn't matter what I wanted. Bruce's, "You had better do as I say," made the choice for me.

I had just turned thirteen, and my puberty was in overdrive. Girls, girls, girls! That's all I thought about. But I was always had to be on high alert for Mom's masturbation patrol marching into my bedroom at night. Even when I wasn't doing anything close to that, she accused me as if I were.

Bruce filled me in on everything I needed to know about girls. Probably way more than I should have known. I was just a curious teenage kid with raging hormones. He knew just how to talk in teen-boy language—giving me all the answers to my questions before I even needed to ask. With a smug attitude, he'd say, "Now, Tom, you will be all prepared for the intimate stuff by the time you start dating girls—you owe me."

I was gullible. His mind control made me think he was doing me a favor in teaching me how to be with a girl. All he was really doing was teaching me how to be with a boy.

But until Bruce said what he said about owing him, I never realized I owed him anything. There was no other choice but to follow his rules. Bruce was the one with the gun—and his gun made the rules.

One silly positive out of all that was that Bruce's bed in his apartment was soft, not like spending the night at his parents' house in the backyard on the hard ground in his tent. Plus, unlike my own home, I liked being able to take a shower there. It was kind of fun acting like I was his roommate. Even if it was just pretend.

One morning; after an overnight at Bruce's apartment, I locked the bathroom door and hopped in the shower. It took a while to get the water warm, but I was finally able to climb in. Rinsing the soap off out of my eyes, I opened them to Bruce's face peeking at me through the shower curtain. *He had to have picked the lock and let himself in.* He pulled back the shower curtain for me to see he was completely in the buff. He wasn't shy of his chunky, hairy gut that stepped over the tub to get in with me—pulling the shower curtain all the way closed behind him.

I'm not shy, so me being naked was not a problem for me; but the thought of what he had in mind was. He asked, "Do you want me to lather you up?" The soap slipped out of his hands and dropped to the bottom of the tub. Bending over, I grabbed for the bar. With a real serious look on his face, Bruce said, "You know what happens to inmates in prison when one guy bends over and picks up the soap, don't you?"

Hesitantly, I said, "Uh, nope."

"It means he wants another guy to have sex with him."

I squeezed my butt muscle cheeks together and backed up against the wall of the shower as fast as I could, and started scrubbing my body. "Uh . . . do you mean my butt hole? If that's what you mean, Bruce, that won't be me. That would hurt so bad. My butt hole is for exit only!"

Bruce yanked the soap out of my hand and roared, almost pushing me. "Get the heck out of the shower." He didn't even let me rinse the suds off. He was so mad, he growled, "I know I told you to never say, 'No,' to me. You just did. Be prepared, Tommy boy, it will happen. You know it will—or else."

He wasn't kidding. Still dripping wet with bubbles all over me, I tried to get my clothes on. The soapy water made my clothes stick to me and I had to wriggle like crazy to get them on before he got out of the shower.

Is he going loony? Why is he so sex-crazed? Why can't he get a woman to do what he wants? Why me? Why me?

I was so nervous, I buttoned up my shirt all catawampus-like; one side of the hem was all crooked. I didn't care. I just pulled my sweatshirt over my head and called it good. He said nothing, just stomped like a toddler passing by me, as I sat hunched over waiting on his loveseat, ready to leave. He wouldn't even look at me—he just grumbled swear words while he kicked the refrigerator door shut. Pulling out of the apartment parking lot, his tires screeched as he swerved in and out of cars like some lunatic, almost smashing into one. Traffic sucked that morning, making me late for school. *Mom's not going to be happy if she finds out. That'll be one strike against Bruce. Should I ask him to write me a note? Maybe I should tell her. Maybe she won't allow me to go back to his apartment anymore because I was late?*

In class, all I could think about was what he meant. I couldn't concentrate on the teacher. *He had never said that to me before. He sounded rude and mean.* In my mind, I could picture what he said about the guys in prison and the bar of soap. *Gross! There is poop up there.*

I skipped practice that day and walked straight home after school. I was in deep thought when I was startled by a groovy looking van pulling up beside me. It was Bruce. I was afraid to look at him. When he rolled down the window to talk to me, his mood had changed to giddy and happy again.

"Where'd your Scout go, Bruce?"

"Oh, I still have it. I thought I would treat myself to this beauty too. Do you like it?"

There were no windows other than the windshield and driver and passenger side doors. I couldn't see in until he rolled the window down to talk to me. I had never seen such dark, tinted windows before—like a mystery van I'd seen in the movies.

"I'm sorry if I scared you this morning . . . about the soap? You do know I was joking?" I wasn't sure if I believed him, but his apology made me feel a little better. "Jaws, the movie, is coming out this Friday at the

drive-in. Would you like to go? What if your brother came with us?"
I often wondered why Bruce didn't hang out with any friends his own
age. Well, I'm sure he was lonely. I hope he knew I would always be his
friend. I immediately said, "Yes, for sure," without even thinking. I was
so thankful he wasn't mad at me, but I would have said yes regardless.

I didn't care what we did or where we went, I just cared that I was
back on his good side. I figured we'd all just have a good old time in the
van, stuffing our faces with popcorn, and all get freaked out together
from watching the movie. If my brother is going to be there, *I'm sure
Bruce won't try anything.*

When Bruce picked us up, Matt screeched, and ran to the front seat.
"I get the front seat."

"You can sit in the back, Tom," Bruce told me.

Reluctantly, I climbed in; giving up my spot. I tried not to frown. *That
passenger seat is reserved for me, and only me—not my brother. I'm Bruce's
only co-pilot.* But, I was not going to let Bruce know I was pouting.

Bruce loaded us up with pizza, popcorn, candy, and a cooler full
of grape and cherry soda. I gorged on the pizza and candy, and guzzled
the pop—enough to get me feeling sick to my stomach. Matt started
to get hyper. I wanted to tell him, "Matt, you are so annoying . . . settle
down." I guess I just really wanted to be with Bruce by myself.

Finally, it was dark enough for the movie previews to start. It would
have made more sense for Bruce to park the van the other way so that
we could open both doors to lounge and watch the movie; all cushioned
by the blankets he piled up back there. But watching the movie wasn't
in Bruce's plan.

When the previews started, Bruce climbed between the seats, and
moved himself to the back of the van. He pulled some black drapes that
hung closed in between the front and the back. He suggested that I move
up to the passenger seat, and let me know, "I need to talk with your
brother to calm him down a bit. I also need you to turn up the volume
on the radio so we can hear the frequency for the movie loud and clear."

I knew it! I'm not clueless—I'm not that stupid.

My butt was planted in the seat, staring face forward at the screen.
I covered my ears to muffle any sounds they might make.

I'm not the only one! I'm not!

My eyes started tearing up, and my heart was pounding. Bruce is such a liar. I was bothered by the amount of time it was taking them back there. Blasting the radio even louder, hoping it would make them hurry up, I started munching on more popcorn, and gulped down the last drop of my third soda to clear the lump in my throat.

It worked. Matt peered through the slit in between the curtains, and nudged me to trade places with him. He slid into the driver's seat for me to get by, and planted his butt in his seat and stared toward the screen the same as I did. We didn't look back and forth at each other at all. Didn't have to. We just knew.

I climbed back behind the curtains to see Bruce lying there under a blanket; sprawled out with his arms up and crossed under his head. Acting like he was some hot dude, he pulled the blanket down to show off his hairy, blubbery chest.

He grabbed the neckline of my t-shirt, and pulled me close toward him. My adrenaline was pumping full blast. As soon as I saw his face, my only emotion was jealousy. Pure jealousy. I could only think, *Bruce is mine. No one else is going to take my Prize Scout position. I've earned it. No one is going to be better than me. I'm the best. If my brother wants a competition, he's got one now. Game on! I'm going to prove to Bruce that this Stewart brother right here is better than that Stewart brother up there.*

Bruce joked with me, "Well, I guess we will need to come back next week to see the movie again, since we have missed almost half of it."

I pulled the curtain open and Bruce moved himself back to the front—trading places with Matt. The only thing I could think about was if I had won the competition. Bruce had never mentioned Matt doing those things with him before. Why would Bruce even need anyone else other than me anyway? Eager to hear the results, Bruce stretched himself in between the seats and leaned back. He cuffed his hand around my earlobe to whisper, "Don't fret, Tom. You are staying in your perfect prized place."

Matt and I didn't speak about what happened that night. As long as I retained my "Prize Favorite" status, Bruce would never need Matt again.

THIRTEEN

FINGERS CROSSED

I WAS MISSING Scouts . . . a lot . . . after almost two years without it, Bruce was running out of excuses for my mom, so he found another troop for me. It just happened to be the same troop he earned his Eagle Scout rank in—Troop 336. He knew the Scoutmaster, so he offered to help out with the troop. Bruce convinced him that he wanted to personally guide me along. Two years out of the Scouts was such a long time, I worried that earning Eagle Scout was a lost cause. Becoming an Eagle Scout was so important to me—more than playing the viola, or any sports I participated in. But, I knew with Bruce's help, I wouldn't fail.

"I want my Prize Scout back by my side in uniform," Bruce proudly said. He was good at making me feel wanted and needed.

I went over the Scout Oath in my mind. Did I remember it?

On my honor, I will do my best to do my duty to God and my country and to obey the Scout Law; to help other people at all times; to keep myself physically strong, mentally awake, and morally straight.

Morally straight? I had a problem when I got to that part. Isn't morally straight the opposite of immorally gay. I knew for sure I was not gay. Because of that, I hated the Bruce stuff. Bruce is keeping me from being morally straight, and forcing me to lie like he does.

Will I eventually turn gay because of how much he has done with me?
Could I still recite the oath if I was not fully telling the truth?

Will I have to hold my hand behind my back with my fingers crossed?
I thought about asking God if that was okay. *Did it count if I was being threatened with a gun?* Maybe God would excuse that one.

What do I do? I had always obeyed my authority—but to do so, I might have to not tell the truth some times. *Which rule do I disobey?*

In Scouts, God is at the forefront. *If I was doing my duty to Him, obeying authority, and following all the other rules, why was God not protecting me from what Bruce was doing to me?*

Looking in the mirror, I had no doubt whatsoever of who was staring back—me, a teenage boy who was as straight as they come . . . except for my teeth, that is. They were about as crooked as they come. Not for long, though. Braces were next on the calendar for Mother to create the perfect Stewart smile. If my glasses and braces weren't enough to label me as a dork, puberty plagued me with a million zits. Mother was determined to solve this. She tried treating me nightly with every acne cream she could buy off the shelf. None of them worked. That was after she almost squeezed my face off to pop the pimples. Off we went to the dermatologist for the latest and greatest procedures. Multiple treatments of lancing with needles, infrared, ultraviolet lights, and even liquid nitrogen. Grueling processes, but I did appreciate Mother's willingness to help me try to avoid the inevitable "crater face" comments.

With glasses, braces, and acne working against me, just being Mr. Nice Guy was not enough to attract the girls. At least during basketball and baseball season, my status went from dork to jock—and I self-taught myself on how to use it to my full advantage. A jock with a 4.0 GPA; willing to help chicks out with their homework?

Brilliant idea. I gave myself an A+ pat on the back when they swarmed all over me.

I soaked up and bathed in my all-star, varsity status. I had to. It was the only thing that allowed me to separate my secret from me. My connection to girls was the only surefire way I could reassure myself that Bruce would not ruin me as a guy.

My girl schemes needed precise planning. When I wore my Scout uniform on meeting days, it worked out just as I had planned. Chicks hovered. Unfortunately, no matter what chick I wanted to date, or invite over to my house, I knew Mother would scare her off in no time. She would have been cast out like a demon with no chance at all against the most protective mother in the universe. How did Bruce's maneuvers slip through her radar?

Thinking about Bruce, he told me that he was moving from his apartment to a house. After I got my braces on, I offered to help him before he even had to ask me. I want to go check out this thing that he is boasting about.

Bruce took me up on my offer to help him—starting with packing . . . packing . . . and more packing. Being a bachelor, he sure had collected some strange stuff.

He asked me to start by filling the empty boxes he had in his bedroom. I was a very neat packer, and this was my thing. In his room, I found some of his hidden treasures—a bunch of dirty magazines. I was so tempted to peek at one, but Mom threatened the wrath of God into me. "If you ever go near one, Thomas Gregory Stewart, you'll go to hell if you do."

What was the deal with Mom anyway? She didn't seem to have a problem with parading around naked. She was the only naked woman I had ever actually seen in the flesh. No concept of modesty. It was just so gross to see my own mother naked.

Maybe that was her strategy to keep me away from girls. Jackhammering in my brain how I needed to stay a virgin until I got married. I hope Bruce didn't count in that area?

Bruce poked his head around the corner of the bedroom door, startling me. I jumped up and started coughing. He walked towards me and said, "It's okay, you can sit down. Hmmm. I think I will join you." Sitting next to me on the bed, he leaned into me with a funny smile, and asked, "Would you like to look at those?" Nothing came out of my mouth. I was more curious than I had ever been before. Bruce had been a teenager once—and I was one now—so he knew, of course, I wanted to. *Naked girls? Sure.* "Go ahead. You know you want to look." I reached for the magazine, and handed it to him. He rustled through a few pages to get to the center, as I looked on in awe. Bruce was acting like he was my instructor. "This is called the centerfold. Notice it's in the center and it's the full length of the magazine. That's where I always look first. Nice, huh?"

I was speechless. He started back at the beginning and went page by page. I was feeling a lot of sensations down there. Maybe Bruce was really trying to teach me something worthwhile. He watched me, seemingly mesmerized looking at the photos with him. It was as if he had a partner in crime. As we turned each page, he was getting antsy and couldn't sit still. His heavy breathing was drifting down my neck. He started grunting softly, and I thought, *Oh, shoot!* We got halfway through the magazine and stopped again at the centerfold. He laid it open-faced on the bed, propped up on the pillow. "I look at this at night, Tom, when I go to bed, fantasizing about me being with her; or any of those girls, for that matter. I need you to do something for me—I am going to close my eyes, lie down, and I want to pretend that you are her." *What is wrong with this guy?*

I picked up the magazine, continuing to look through, trying to hold off, as long as I could.

He darted up to shout at me, "Tom, what did I tell you?" *Well, I had better get this over with. But, my mouth was hurting so bad.* There were so many cuts in my cheeks from my new braces.

Bruce lay back on the bed, closed his eyes again, and waited. His usual annoying shakes and squirms and moans and groans suddenly turned into a loud screech of "Ow!" Followed by a bunch of swear words. I launched backwards, scared at what I might have done.

"Your braces, Tom, they hurt like hell! Look! Do you see what you did?"

My heart was pounding as fast as it ever had. "I'm sorry . . . I'm sorry, Bruce." My braces had nicked his penis in a couple of spots and he was bleeding.

I tried hard to wipe the smile off my face. Luckily, he was scrunched up into a little ball; whimpering.

Who's the "wussy" now?

Ha! I bet he won't ask for that again, as long as I have these defense mechanisms in my mouth!

I would take the taste of blood in my mouth over the salty taste of his satisfaction any day. Even my mouth sores feel better not having to gag on him.

He didn't seem to be as angry with me as I expected. He must either be really embarrassed, or really be in pain. *That'll teach him.*

As he left the room holding his privates, he mumbled at me to keep on packing. Those dirty magazines filled the entire box to the top.

"What about the furniture?" I asked, looking around. Bruce sounded annoyed I had even asked. "We only need the mattress tonight. The rest of the furniture won't fit with all the boxes in there. I will come back for the furniture after I'm done with you . . . uh . . . I mean . . . uh . . . after we unload."

I heard what he said, and knew what he meant, but my braces won't be going near him any time soon. Bruce carries his protection . . . I carry mine. I was free from worrying about doing that for a long, long time. With the van now full, Bruce said, "Let's get a move on. I'm sure traffic's not going to give us a break today."

When we arrived at his new house, it was disappointing. I was expecting something spectacular the way he had boasted about it. It was dumpy. I thought his apartment was much better. I went ahead and complimented him anyhow.

After we unpacked the load of boxes into the garage, I helped him carry the mattress in to the middle of the living room floor. "We can sleep out here tonight."

I didn't know if he deliberately kept his twin-sized bed for a reason. It left only enough room for him to lie behind me with his arm wrapped around me just like in his little two-man tent. For dinner, Bruce ordered pizza to be delivered. Sitting on the mattress, Bruce thanked me for helping him move. Especially the big, heavy girlie magazine box. "It's my most precious cargo. Now, I'm sure you understand why." Me knowing him, there could only be one way he was going with this.

"I want to sit down with you and look at the other ones we haven't had to chance to go through yet."

Very interested, Bruce wanted to know, "What questions do you have about girls, Tom?"

I shrugged and shoved more pizza in my mouth. I didn't want to talk about anything referring to girls. That would just lead him to talking about how he would teach me how to have sex with a girl. Which then would lead him to only I know what.

Bruce drove me home the next morning without making any more advances toward me at all. That surprised me. The cuts from my braces must have still been bothering him. I knew full well how the braces hurt my mouth and made it bleed. I could only imagine how it felt down there.

Staring out the passenger seat window, I knew the first thing I was going to do . . . *I am going to find Mother, and give her a big hug and thank her for wanting to fix my crooked teeth.* She'd have no idea what I was really thanking her for.

Dropping me off in the driveway, Bruce confirmed, "Same time next week? We have to celebrate your big one-four . . . you know." I couldn't think of any excuses fast enough before he decided for me. "Okay then."

I stepped in the front door of the house, and leaned against it to shut it. I have been waiting for this day. If all it took was braces to make him stop making me do that, I will gladly endure the cuts and canker sores. *Thank you, Lord, for ailing me with those crooked teeth so I needed to get braces. I will never complain about them again.*

The following weekend, I couldn't wait to see what he had planned for us two guys for my birthday. With all the gross stuff out of the way, I was looking forward to it.

Getting back to his place, he managed to move the rest of his furniture. It was definitely a bachelor pad with his television sitting on a sturdy apple box across from the tiny, faded loveseat under the window.

After using the bathroom, I walked out in the hall and paused for a second. I was tempted to head to my left. That's where his bedroom was, and that's where the magazines were. I had been daydreaming all week about the nudie pictures he had shown me. My hormones were taking over and thinking for themselves. Looking back to the right, I didn't realize that Bruce was studying me from the living room. I'm sure he knew why I was standing there.

He headed toward me and led me to his bedroom. I just followed right behind. His dresser, bed, and nightstand were set up the same way he had it in his apartment. And, where did my eyes sprint to? Exactly. Straight to the nightstand drawer. I wished I had x-ray vision to see if he had unpacked them yet.

Bruce stepped back over by me. "I know what you are waiting for. You want to look, don't you, Tom? They are all unpacked and ready for your viewing pleasure."

Duh! Wanting to look at naked girls in full color?

Not waiting for my answer, he went right for the nightstand and scattered his collection all over the bed. I forgot how many there were—quite the bonanza for a teenager.

I sat down on the floor and he started handing them down to me; one by one.

"Happy Birthday weekend, Tom. Isn't this the best birthday present you have ever had?"

I was a kid in hog heaven. But I heard Mom's voice in my head, nagging, "Uh, no you don't . . . You can't . . . You won't . . . Not allowed, Thomas Gregory Stewart!" I opened one and recognized that it was the one I had looked at before. Grabbing a second one, it had a pretty brunette on the cover. Bruce showed me how to handle the magazine like a real man. "Here, Tom, hold it up in the air, pivot it sideways so the centerfold falls open for a full view." The next magazine he handed me was called *'Twisted Sisters.'* It was not like the other magazines. When the centerfold fell open, it was not what I was expecting at all. I tried to be cool and not be too taken aback by the way the one woman and two men in the picture were posing.

Bruce studied my baffled face. "I told you I wanted to show you more pleasure. Remember me telling you that? Do you realize how lucky you are, my Prize Scout, that you have me to show you these things?"

Nothing surprised me with Bruce. Except for this time. There was a vacuum cleaner in the picture, being using in ways I had never imagined in my wildest dreams.

He said, "I have a woman friend who is willing to come on over and reenact that pose for us. Do you see how we resemble the two men who are in the picture? That'll be us."

I couldn't take my eyes away from the quirky scene.

Bruce said, "My fantasies are coming to life, Tom. Thank you for being my Prize Partner."

Gee, I sure hope he doesn't mean that type of partner.

The sexual pictures got me excited on my own; but his build-up to the scene somehow convinced me this was normal, then enticed me enough to agree.

Bruce left the room for a minute, and came back rolling his big, clunky Hoover vacuum cleaner.

I guess he is serious.

"We can't do anything until you strip." I didn't hesitate, like I usually did. I knew I was safe from doing what I most dreaded—thanks to my braces.

By the time he got the cord unwound from the vacuum, I stood buck naked in the middle of the floor. He convinced me we needed to practice before this mysterious woman came over. Bruce brushed his hand down over my eyelids to close them. He moved my arms over to my sides and out of the way. I could hear him pushing the vacuum closer to me. I had one name for Bruce right then—adventurous. "Curious Tom" and "Adventurous Bruce." I kind of felt privileged, being the chosen one to help him discover his unique side. Even though I was leery on how perverted this was, I have to admit that I was quite curious as to how it was going to feel. I sure wish he would have tried it on himself first.

There was nothing else mentioned about the woman. Knowing Bruce, the picture had to be a decoy for what he wanted to do with me alone.

He knelt down in front of me. "You know what the vacuum is for, right?" I nodded, trying not to open my eyes. I didn't doubt he would actually do what they were doing in the picture, but my privates had their own idea in mind and decided to shrivel up on me.

"Here is our assignment, my Prize Scout. You may open your eyes now and watch. All men want to have a bigger one—we are going to use this vacuum to accomplish that for you and me. We will keep a measurement tally of our progress."

"Besides, I've heard that it feels great."

Then he looked at me and joked, "I'm glad they have this small nozzle attachment for you, Tom. It seems you have shrunk."

I smirked, never dreaming what was next.

I shuddered as his hand grabbed what he could of my penis. My body jerked as he placed the cold, hard nozzle of the vacuum hose over it. He didn't hesitate to flip the on switch. I jolted straight up, and covered my mouth so I wouldn't yell out. It yanked full blast with extreme suction. It was a Hoover after all! I reached over and whacked the off switch. Holding back my tears, I pulled the hose off me. With my penis hanging there, he cackled at my humiliation. "Well; just looky there, Tommy has a flappy, turkey gobbler for a penis. It literally sucked you good."

I tried to force out a laugh to humor him, while struggling not to cry.

Not wanting to look down, the pain made me. I was all disfigured. He told me it was going to be fun. His perverted side made me leery more than ever before.

Miserable where I stood, *what could possibly be worse than this?*

FOURTEEN

OR ELSE!

IT HAD TAKEN about four days for me to return to looking somewhat normal down there. Bruce had thought it was so funny. It wasn't. Quite possibly, it was his sick idea for payback for the pain of my braces. I guess I will never know. The red marks were still there—reminding me of what looked like a hickey. Virgil and I had tried it on our own arms once. Those, too, took a heck of a while to fade. Of course, I had never done that to a girl. First off, Mother would maim me. Then, second, she would maim the girl. The boys I know who have done it told me they do it to stake their claim on their girl—like their tagged property.

I am surprised Bruce hasn't yet sucked a hickey on me to leave his mark on his prize boy toy.

I tried to keep my mind off everything, except how to come up with an excuse not to go back to his house. I may have been book smart, but . . . oh boy . . . Bruce was the one who could outsmart everyone, including me.

How can I tell Mother that I don't want to go over there anymore? I went to my Scout meeting that Monday, and Bruce was there of course, masquerading in his usual leading role. Nothing was said about the weekend coming up. I thought I might get lucky and be free from him. *Who am I kidding?*

On Saturday, when Mom brought me home from my viola lesson, his black van was just sitting in my driveway. *He is not even asking if I want to go anymore—he just shows up unannounced.*

Mother said to me, "You must be a great help to Bruce over at his new place, eh, Tom?"

With my head resting against the window, I kept it there and didn't want to look up. But I did. And there he was, stepping out of his van to greet my mom.

Bruce headed straight toward my mom, "Hello, Mrs. Stewart, you look beautiful today, as always." When my eyes met his, he gave me his usual head nod. All I could see in that head nod was a liar with a sick mind. I can't stomach the sight of him anymore. No matter how much he had helped me and had done for me, I knew he was just a nasty sicko underneath it all.

Mother didn't even ask if I wanted to go. She just shooed me inside to get what I needed so I could go with him.

I tried. "Mom, I was planning on hanging out with Virgil today." It didn't work. Her dreaded you-better-not-back-talk-me look answered that one. "Bruce didn't drive all the way down here for you to be rude, Thomas Gregory Stewart."

Dragging my feet and my viola toward the house, I whispered a prayer. "God, why me? Please help me. Please make Bruce stop." *Why was God not hearing me?*

Heading back outside with my backpack, I passed Mother with a fly-by kiss and a weak, "Love you."

In Bruce's cunning manner, he said, "I can drop him off tomorrow morning before church, Mrs. Stewart, if that's okay?"

Without a clue, she happily thanked him. "Of course, Bruce. Thank you for taking such good care of my son."

I upchucked a little bit just to swallow it again.

The entire drive, I said nothing. Bruce tried to make small talk. I wanted nothing to do with it. He parked in his driveway and waited for me to look at him. I couldn't. I got out and walked to the front door, head down. Once he shut the door, I went over to the love seat. Strange vibes were blaring off him. I couldn't help but look up; it was as if he was drawing me in. His eyes felt like laser beams pulling me into almost a hypnotic state—which I had come to recognize as shutting down.

"Tom, stop with the poor-me routine and get out of your pity party, boy." In a gruff voice, he threatened me with what was so important to me. "If you want to remain my Prize Scout, wipe that pathetic frown off your face and get some happy back into you."

His frustration seemed to be escalating, "Didn't you like how the vacuum felt? Don't you appreciate anything I do for you?"

Cowering down my face, I heard the deadbolt lock the front door. Bruce never lifted his feet up when he walked. Without looking up, I could tell when he went from the carpet to the bathroom tile. The door shut. I knew I had to rush, so I quietly rose up and tiptoed over to the kitchen to find a knife or scissors or something to cut that stupid cord on the vacuum. I sure didn't want to go through that again.

He was not the nice Bruce today. It was like there was some strange dark cloud over him. It felt like evil in that house. Before I could even slide one of the kitchen drawers open, I peeked really quick behind me and shrieked. Just like a horror flick, there he was, the boogeyman hovering over his victim. I was scared out of my wits. He took three steps backward without even blinking and stiffly lifted his arm to point me to walk toward the hall. I heeled at my master's command. Right behind me, he tailed me to the bedroom. Bruce immediately whisked the curtains closed. My body went cold and my hands were clammy. Bruce brushed next to me and reached for the doorknob to shut the door. I waited as the seconds went by to see what move he would make next. My feelings were blank. I just felt empty, as if every part of me had bled out.

Without even thinking, I begged, "Bruce, please, can we stop what we are doing?"

I should have known that was a huge mistake.

His nostrils flared. He almost spat his anger in my face. His fist raised up like he was going to hit me. Then he reached behind his back and grabbed for his gun tucked where he always had it, in the waistband of his pants. He swung the gun around to give me a close-up view of his threat. His thumb clicked off the safety before he placed it on the nightstand.

He sat down on the bed, folded his arms, and the drill sergeant commands began. "You can start with taking off your shirt. Not just any old way—the way I tell you to. I expect you to start out slowly. Look at me while you are doing it—like you are doing a sexy strip tease for me."

I paused and looked at him as if I were asking, "Are you kidding me?"

This guy is truly whacked! Bruce grabbed for the gun off the nightstand and laid it on the bed next to him. I was shaking so hard I couldn't do the sexy moves the way he wanted. I tried to stay focused and do what he said, but I couldn't. All I saw was the gun.

As I pulled my shirt off my head, Bruce pulled his shirt off. With every move that I made, he would do the same. He told me to come over and undo his belt for him, and he would undo mine at the same time.

Bruce recited what he wanted me to say to him, "Oh, Bruce, you are my sexy, hot lover." *Uh, that's not going to come out of my mouth.*

He slid his gun over to the center of the bed. I froze. I wouldn't be able to do the dirty talk thing to him right now even if I did try.

He raised his hips to push his pants down to encircle his ankles. "Slowly slide your pants down inch by inch, Tom. You excite me!" I was grossed out by the sight of him as he started to play with himself.

Dirty sayings were falling out of his mouth, while his eyes faded in and out, as if he was flying to outer space.

With a twisting movement of my hips, I attempted to do what he said . . . *I hope I'm doing this right.* His "ooh-aah" panting confirmed I was.

I reminded myself that him being mad would not be a good thing right now.

Whatever makes him happy will keep his hand away from that gun.

My pants were down and wrapped around my ankles like his were. He gestured me to turn around, so he could see my rear-end when I bent over to pull my pants off of each foot. Bruce flung his feet up together so I could slide his off too. Naked boy and naked man. *This is so wrong.*

He sat there with his fat belly and an obvious erection. *This grosses me out!* I felt nauseous, but grateful that my braces would keep me from having to do to him what I hated. He moved his gun back over onto the nightstand and cocked it, making sure I saw him do it. He boldly kicked our pile of clothes out of the way. Both of his hands reached out toward mine and grabbed hold to start massaging my palms. He pulled me towards him in a sort of back-and-forth dance move. *Is he trying to seduce me? Is that what he tries with girls? No wonder he doesn't have a girlfriend.* Bruce tightened his grip on my hands and used me to pull himself up to stand toe-to-toe with me.

None of this excited me in the least. I was no homosexual. He let go of my hands, and wrapped his fingers hard around my arms.

Our face-to-face did a 180-degree turn and switched places. His intense grip was hurting me; he wasn't easing up. There are going to be red marks on my arms now too.

He then tilted his head sideways and raised his eyebrows toward the gun on the nightstand. Harshly shaking my body, scowling with a hellish-sound, "Do you see that gun? That gun that is loaded and cocked?"

I was trapped. My shins were in between him and the bed. One of his hands eased off a little bit to let go and spin me around to face the bed, repositioning me so that the front side of him spooned the back side of me pinning me in place. His palms seized both of my shoulder blades and forced me forward; down flat on the bed, face-first into the sheets. My legs flew up in between where his legs were planted; wedging me in and lodging me where he wanted me.

I felt him creeping over me. His fat stomach smashed into my back first, and the rest of his blubber squished into me.

He was so heavy, I couldn't breathe. I couldn't move. I couldn't think. I just wanted to scream. But who would hear me? No one!

With his heavy breathing and bad breath blowing on the back of my neck, I had to turn my head to the side to get some air. He was drooling.

My ear was so close to the demands of his rough voice. "You have seen my gun, and I have given you fair warning. You do what I say and what I want, and you will not get hurt. If you disobey or try and run,

I will aim . . . fire . . . and shoot you. Then, I will be heading for your family next."

I couldn't even speak to say, "Yes, Sir."

The only thing that was moving about was my adrenaline. I believed him. He wasn't kidding. With my arms held flat on each side of me, Bruce pushed his body up and back and away from me. This allowed me to at least breathe again. Doing what I did best, I lay low and kept quiet. I felt his hands grab my hips and pull me close to the edge of the bed, where my waist bent off and down the side so my feet hit the floor. He adjusted me to where he wanted me. Dread overwhelmed me. I knew what was coming. There was nothing I could do. *Just kill me,* I thought. But I was so scared for my family.

I inhaled so deep and held it as long as I could.

Bruce boosted my hips up to position them to his height. He started to drag his front side around my backside. Grabbing a hold of the thighs of my legs, I squeezed my rear end together as hard as I could so he couldn't do what he told me what happens back there. I was still squeezing with all my might when I felt him starting to press himself harder against me. Letting go of one side of me, with his open hand, he slapped the cheek of my butt . . . so hard, I released my straining hold.

His movements intensified. He knew exactly what he was doing and just how to get there. I was terrified. Speaking through some sporadic inhales and exhales, he reminded me of the gun. He didn't have to; that's where my eyes were looking already.

There was the sudden sensation of pressure. It was starting to build. His thrusting slowly continued inward. The pain was intensifying, and elevated to the unimaginable. My emotional pain inside was shattering.

I tried to bite the sheets to gag my wailing, but it didn't help. He kept on going. He didn't care. Nothing was going to stop him. That was my last thought before I must have blacked out.

I thought I had died. I wished I had. But, the sound of a door slamming jolted me out from under the sheets. I frantically gasped for air, but quickly shut myself up since Bruce had to be near.

Getting my bearings, I wasn't sure how long I was out.

The sheets were soaking wet. I was chilled. I freaked out when I saw it wasn't just sweat. There was blood all over. I panicked, and couldn't think straight.

Shivering, I slowly walked to the bathroom to clean myself up. It hurt to move. *It hurts so bad.* All I could do was squeeze my muscles down there to ease the throbbing.

I propped one hand up against the wall while using the toilet, as the tears started pouring down my cheeks. In disbelief, I thought, *Did this really happen to me?* The pain and mess tell me it did. Whispering through my sobbing, "I've been raped."

I never thought a man would do that to a boy.

FIFTEEN

NO VOICE, NO CHOICE

COUNTLESS NIGHTS WERE tormented by a rerun of Bruce's gun aimed at me through my nightmares, ending with his vulgar acts of sodomy that haunted me through the rest of the night. I desperately sought sleep, but dreaded when the dreams might hit. When I would finally doze off, I would immediately wake up in a frantic state, realizing I wasn't really dreaming. Or was I? There he'd be, standing right behind me with his entitlement, controlling me as if he owned me. The dreams were just a reenactment of the real thing—and the real thing was just a reenactment of the dreams. My role had advanced to being Bruce's own prize sex slave. There were times I couldn't decipher the difference between my triggered visions and reality. At any moment, they would sneak up on me. They were all compounded by the torture called Bruce.

To this day, bedtime is something I don't want to think about. It's like preparing myself to walk into a danger zone. Being able to even drift off to sleep is only part of it. Following a strict routine is the only thing that gives me just enough strength to get myself into bed in the first place. My nightly regimen begins with shutting all doors, as if I am attempting to keep the risk of Bruce's evil locked out. A large, noisy fan next to my bed has to be turned on high to drown out any sudden noises that could remind me of Bruce's approach. Earplugs have become my reinforcements for the fan to make sure no noise cuts through. Otherwise, Bruce's voice might, and then wake me, or prevent me from falling asleep altogether. My digital alarm clock had to be turned completely the other way so I cannot see the large red numbers. Watching each minute tick takes me back to Bruce's bedroom where time stood still until he was done. Counting the minutes, turns into counting hours if I gaze at it long enough.

With my eye mask slung over my forearm, I make sure not to bend over and crawl in bed like normal people do. I am too paranoid Bruce might secretly be hovering behind me ready to pounce. Instead, I came up with a way to shuffle my feet around, backing up so the back of my legs nestled up against the mattress, enabling me to sit down and inch my way under the covers. I wrap myself into my heavy comforter—tucked in and tightly swaddled, I feel it'll keep him from getting close to me, just in case he sneaks into my room late at night through my window.

A daunting routine, but necessary to keep my triggers at bay.

Every week of every month, he'd seek me out to take advantage with his "or else" threats. He stole my ability to speak; he stole my voice. He stole my choice.

I felt permanently choked tighter than any noose. My desperate pleas for mercy were deeply embedded in his mattress, intertwined with that forbidden "no" word that was too scared to be spoken. Just the way Mother taught me.

I lost count after about the fortieth time he sodomized me. All that was by the time I was just fifteen. By seventeen and a half, I struggled to keep myself sane. I threw myself deeper into my already stringent schedule of school, sports, the symphony, and Scouts.

I felt so stupid . . . him being able to do that to me. Him threatening to kill my family made it impossible to do anything but comply. My duty to keep my family safe was the only thing I didn't feel stupid about. My family might have been a most dysfunctional piece of work, but his threats to harm them terrified me. It was up to me; and only me, to protect them in the only way I knew how . . . by taking it.

The chilling words he churned in my ears burned into my soul. *"If you disobey me . . . or run . . . I will aim . . . fire . . . shoot!"*

I felt bound, gagged, tied, and cuffed. My way of evading the obvious was to push and shove my way through with what I had left of me.

Never wanting to second-guess God, there were times I couldn't help myself. I was growing weary and weaker each time Bruce took advantage of me. I prayed, asked, begged, and pleaded for God to take this horrible man away from me. *Why is He not answering me?*

Before I knew it, junior year was under my belt. It left the summer open to concentrate on obtaining Eagle Scout. With a two-year lapse from Scouts, I really had to hoof it. I wasn't sure if it was even possible. But it was either that or face my mother with something she would consider a massive failure.

I felt alone; I was an onlooker, sacrificing all friendships. I didn't have time for friends. Too much to do to complete what was missing.

I hadn't come this far to just let it slide out from underneath me. Of course, Bruce was right there by my side to make it happen. Whatever his motives were, I needed him to help me regardless. That was the side of Bruce I liked—the fun Bruce. I focused on that part of him; it made it easier to overlook his dark side.

My spotty appreciation for Bruce evidenced my brainwashed thinking. As it was, I was fooling myself. Virgil was basically my only friend. I tricked my heart into thinking Bruce was actually another. He was more like an imaginary friend. Anyone with a mother like I had probably had one too.

Mother's intolerance to failure ran me into the ground. That's where I fell back on Bruce. He was my guarantee . . . my buffer . . . my shield. Because of that, dealing with his illicit activities became somewhat tolerable. They had to be. At least he was predictable. I knew just how long I would have to endure it, and then it would be over. On the contrary, Mother's belittling did not cease at just once a week.

I was getting to the home stretch. The sooner I accomplished Eagle Scout, it would be one less pain in my butt as far as her heckling was concerned.

Mother did help seek out and find what my Eagle Scout project was going to be. I appreciated that. She met with the firemen at the local fire station and learned their building needed repainting. An ideal opportunity for an Eagle Scout project for sure. Mother never admitted that her motive was to see a tribute plaque of recognition mounted in the front with the words, "Courtesy of the Stewarts."

Confirmed and certified, *I did it!* I earned my Eagle Scout rank. Bruce ended up speaking at my Eagle Scout Court of Honor Ceremony. He draped me with compliments in front of everyone. He introduced me as his "Prize Scout." The other Scouts in the room looked on and clapped with envy. How one Scout could be so lucky to have a Scout leader take such an interest in a kid like me and take him the distance as Bruce did. They had no idea. Bruce showed me off like I was his shiny trophy. Now that I think about it, I guess that's what I am . . . his prize trophy. The longer I stood next to him and the microphone, the more my journey to get there came back to me. Bruce had me model my sash full of badges. Pointing to each one, he explained how I earned them—badge by badge. For me, the way it resonated in my head sounded quite different from the way he was telling everyone else: *This swimming badge was earned in the locker room. That archery badge was earned in his tent. The camping badge was earned in his back yard* . . . and so on. When Bruce handed me the official Eagle Scout certificate, my painted-on smile turned for

Mother's picture opportunity. Him shaking my hand was an outward acknowledgment for achieving the Eagle Scout rank. Me shaking his hand was an inward acknowledgment to myself—*against all odds . . . even with what he did to me, I did it. Thank you, Lord. I can do anything.*

Into my senior year, my schedule got even more insane. My regimen with Scouts had been replaced with what Mother had been waiting for since before kindergarten . . . where this Stewart would attend college. I plowed into college applications, traveling to prestigious universities of her choice for me, and taking multiple entrance exams and SAT tests. This became my senior year social life. I guess it was hers as well.

Confused, I staggered back and forth between being thankful and being resentful. With my mother, I had come to the point of being thankful for her giving me the drive to keep up with it all.

With Bruce, resentment blanketed my view; yet, me being dumbfounded was more like it. I could never figure out why a man would choose to be with a boy in the first place.

All of this has to eventually come to halt sometime, doesn't it?

Whatever college I decided to attend, I knew the distance between Mother and me would replenish some of my missing peace of mind. But, more importantly, I leaned on what I did have left, knowing Bruce couldn't follow me there.

SIXTEEN

YELLOW TASSELS

ODDLY ENOUGH, BRUCE'S association with me had begun to ease off. Now that Scouts was off my schedule, he must have lost interest in me. With my "tell it like it is" sarcasm, I wondered if little boys were his favorite flavor on the menu because he wasn't very well endowed. Besides my attempt to laugh it off, I prayed, "Dear God, please, please keep him away from any other little boys."

Mother revved her engines and did whatever it took to maintain my superior Stewart status in the high school's select top ten seniors. She was relentless with her need to see me acquire an infinite amount of scholarships, awards, recognitions, medals, and honors.

Without Bruce lurking right behind me, filling out all the paperwork about me and my accomplishments, forced me to take a good, hard-pressed look at myself. It forced me to open myself up to just how deeply troubled I was about my sexuality. That was difficult. I had been so entangled by Bruce's use of me that I had not caught up with myself after puberty.

He left me no opportunity to be an actual teenage boy.

Programmed by Mother's constant hell and damnation warnings at a young age, I had walled off that part of my thought life because it was all considered dirty. Bruce only confused my already mixed-up understanding of what normal was.

She couldn't know I wasn't her perfect virgin boy anymore. Betty Lou would have damned me to hell if I was responsible for tarnishing the high and mighty Stewart name. But, there was no one I could talk to about it or confide in—making me that much more curious about obsessing with girls. *Am I the only one who is this girl-crazy?* I couldn't and wouldn't stop fantasizing about them. The thoughts about being with a girl were nonstop, all the time. That was the only feeling that felt normal to me. All I could thank him for was how clear he made it that I was not like him.

The only one-on-one experience I had up until then was at a couples' dance at the elaborate holiday cotillion with a nerdy girl from the school orchestra. Mom already bought the tickets, so I had to find someone. It took all my guts to ask a classmate of mine. She happened to play the viola like me. Mom's perfect match—a violist and a violist.

I was so nervous. Mother made sure I dressed in my best—the dignified symphony tux with a bow tie I used for orchestra concerts.

That first experience left me sitting alone at the table for most of the night, waiting for my date to come out of the bathroom. We didn't even dance. No words were said, and only awkward silence all the way home. It was a disaster. Needless to say, the goodnight kiss I was waiting for flopped like our date did.

Driving home, I wanted to quit orchestra before I had to face the girl on Monday. I hadn't dared ask if she wanted to go out with me again. Completely nerdy and geeky me. Feeling totally rejected, I wallowed in how Bruce must be branded all over my face.

Time to snap out of it, Tom. I didn't have time to think about any of that right then. My focus needed to change to what was ahead of me. Mother's plans for my success were right on target, and scheduled for takeoff. I was to be the perfect graduate with the much-desired recognition she'd been hoping for.

Down in the basement at my little corner of the Ping-Pong table, I had completed the multiple applications per Mother's requests.

Neatly addressed, stamped and stacked, ready to mail.

What else I discovered from looking deep inside myself was how I; myself, had been in denial as a rebellious son in regards to Mother. Looking at the stack of what my future might hold, I can't argue that what I am sending out is a byproduct of her relentless pushing. I had never thought about it in that way before.

Her drive fueled me all along. In a bittersweet sense, she encouraged me and steered me by exasperating me to find my own purpose. I had learned to tune out her voice that had become white noise to me. That gave me a technique and ability to concentrate, focus, and bury myself in my school work no matter what was going on around me. I wondered if she realized her intimidating behavior actually did me a favor.

My entire senior year was a whirlwind. All that constant preparation fast-forwarded me to my upcoming graduation. I was so exhausted that I didn't even go to prom. No time and no date for me anyway. I was so devastated after my first date fail, I purposely concocted my beset excuse to get me out of going at all. On graduation day, Mother emptied an entire roll of film of me dressed in my graduation cap and gown. The yellow-braided honor tassels and the gold-colored, medal honor medallion around my neck told me again: *against all odds, I did it.*

To the audience, they told a different story. Denoted as the perfect scholar, hand-raised by Robert and Betty Lou. An all-American kid born in ideal circumstances.

As the procession began, my class of 1981 walked in alphabetical order to "Pomp and Circumstance" in an auditorium filled to the rafters. Mom got her wish. I was honored to sit on stage as one of the top ten with honors, among the top twenty best of them. The hundreds of other graduates outfitted in either yellow or blue caps and gowns took their places on the floor.

No one could miss my parents tirelessly waving their programs in the air. I'm sure Mother would have liked to be sitting right up there on stage with me. Were they really proud of me? Or was it just the old Stewart pride making sure everyone noticed that they were the ones who had the son with the word "valedictorian" imprinted beside his name?

I stared off into the bright lights on the ceiling in a rare moment of reflection. As I sat there, glimpses of a very long and lonely path replayed in my mind. After the announcements, the speeches, and the music, it was time for the honor awards. We honor students on the stage were told to rise. My heart started pounding. I glanced back out at my parents. They seemed giddy as they again waved at me and snapped more pictures. Proud parents soaking it up. Isn't that what we are supposed to do . . . make our parents proud?

The principal announced the honors, awards, and scholarships that defined our overachieving, hard work. When he came to my name, it took awhile for him to get through the list:

Top Ten Honor Medal
WA State Principal's Scholar List
University of Washington Fraternity Scholarship
University of Washington Academic Scholarship
Full scholarship at University of Arizona
Full scholarship at University of Utah
First place in Elks scholarship
The Bernice A. B. Keyes Scholarship
Kiwanis Club Leadership Award
The Richard Graff Award for Fair Play and Clean Performance
Inspirational Award
Senior Chief Carr Award
Senior Science Achievement Award

All City and lettered in varsity basketball
All City and lettered in varsity baseball and Coach's Award
National Bureau for the Achievement of Music Award

My cheeks warmed from blushing a bit, but I was humbled by the warm applause.

Sitting back down, I studied the program. It was as if I had to see it on paper to believe it. It wasn't the list of achievements that I was in awe about, it was all I made it through to get here.

As the awarding of diplomas began, there was ongoing clapping, whistling, and shout-outs from the families who came out to cheer on their graduates. My name was next. Hearing "Thomas Gregory Stewart" had me thanking God for where I was standing. Reaching out with my right hand for the handshake, receiving my diploma with the other, I knew my smile for the camera was genuine this time. My watery eyes told me that the emotions were not completely gone. *Thank you, Lord, for getting me here. I think I'm going to be okay.*

Time to turn our tassels. It was unbelievably freeing to toss my cap into the air along with the rest of the graduating class of 1981.

Something had eased in me during this rite of passage. My bitterness for Mother was slowly deflating like a popped balloon. Her pounded-in demands for perfection had left no room for less. I had been honored because of it.

That bubble of thankfulness for my mother sprang open something resembling forgiveness in me. It was life-changing in itself.

SEVENTEEN

SWEATING BULLETS

AS AN OFFICIAL high school graduate, my decision of where I wanted to attend college was made: The University of Washington. Blessed with scholarships, I was pumped. I had three months to go before I was set to leave. Mom was thrilled I chose a local college; still close enough for her to come visit and continue to control me at her whim. *Just gotta love that mother of mine.*

When the time would come for me to move to a dorm on campus, it would allow me the much-needed space I never had. I never had a chance to spread my wings without Mother's clipping. A little apprehensive, I wasn't sure how well I'd fit into the college scene; my reclusive manner held me back from stepping out. I was told what to expect from college life, but none of that partying stuff I heard about was going to be for me. I don't think Mother realized how lucky she was to have a teenager who never disobeyed, never smoked, never drank, never swore, or never even got into any trouble.

No matter how much I thought I wanted to fit in, I didn't falter. It's funny. In junior high and high school, it was cool to be bad to the bone. Yet to some, the brainy, church kid can be the outcast. Today, I am grateful I was that outcast.

Having been nonstop scheduled as far back as I could remember, I woke up early the day after graduation not knowing what to do with myself. I didn't even remember the last time I had slept in. I lay there looking over at my diploma when it dawned on me, *Bruce wasn't there last night.* The last several months that Mother had me so thoroughly occupied, Bruce stopped calling. Then he stopped coming by altogether. My subconscious must have got so used to shutting him out of my mind when I wasn't with him, I must have shut him out completely without even trying.

I didn't feel upset about it. In fact, I didn't feel anything. What I did feel was an absence of stress. Did that mean the threat to my family was also over?

Haven't seen hide nor hair of him. *Are we out of harm's way? Oh, Lord, please!*

Sadly, there was no way that I could have been the only one. He was too much of a sicko to stop with just me. But there was also no possible way that anyone else could have been as gullible as I was.

I kept beating myself up. *Tom, you were just plain old naïve and dumb.* Remembering back to the time my brother Matt and I went with Bruce to the drive-in. After the fact, I was envious of how much smarter Matt was than me—smart enough to get away and keep his distance away from Bruce, before he sunk his claws in him for keeps. Without a doubt, I had to be his only stupid Scout.

Eventually, I would have to tell Mother what happened, but I wasn't ready to do that yet. I needed to move forward and begin the process of cleansing myself of him.

Since Dad was head of personnel at the American Plywood Association, he had connections in the industry who helped me get a summer job as a factory worker at a chemical plant. My duties at the end of the production line had me standing at the brunt-end of the conveyor belt, catching fifty pound bags of wood preservative flakes called pentachlorophenol. I would be the backstop when they slid down the chute to be sealed up for shipment. I had to be on high alert to not get sucker punched in the gut for not paying attention to what was coming my way. Sealing and stacking the bags on pallets was a strenuous and brutal, nonstop job.

Good thing I had some stamina and endurance from sports. There were stringent safety precautions due to the conditions. Employees were required to wear safety glasses, protective coveralls, arm guards, and gloves at all times. It was especially hot that summer, and wearing all that gear made it feel like I had a sauna wrapped around me. The airborne odors and flying dust made me feel loopy so I couldn't focus. Other responsibilities of mine involved vacuuming out the furnace that become lined with a heavy powder. Then, finish off by cleaning out the formaldehyde liquid pits.

At the end of each work day, I was drenched with sweat, almost to the point of dehydration. It was the hardest job I have ever done, but I kept plugging along. My dad had helped me get it, so whining or complaining was not allowed. Besides, I didn't want it to be me who might have given Dad a bad name for referring me.

Since I was tall in stature, sometimes the protective clothing would not cover all of me. Parts of my extremities would be exposed to the toxic chemicals the gear was supposed to protect us from. The toxins absorbed into my skin like a sponge. I didn't think anything of it, just wiped it off and continued earning my pay.

Even after showering at home, the sweat continued to pour out. I had no doubt that it was the heat of the summer, so I chose to sleep in the basement where it was cooler.

I hauled my sleeping apparatuses from my bedroom down the stairs, so adjusting to a different place to sleep wouldn't affect me too much. I was praying that it wouldn't anyway. Just because I wanted all the triggers to go away didn't make it so. After all, that basement is where Bruce abused me; where the stench of his lingering odor didn't allow me to brush off the flashbacks that came with being down there.

Eventually, I'd would wake up several times a night drenched in sweat with the sheets soaking wet. It felt like I was at the plant in my astronaut type suit, even though I was at home in my underwear. I'd awake in a state of deliriousness—not conscious of where I was at first; drowsy with the same loopy feeling I had at work. If I did happen to fall back asleep, I would drift straight into a nightmare with Bruce; waking up again, begging God to help me get back to sleep again. It was strange though, I dripped more sweat down in that basement than I ever did on the production line. I continued to sweat like crazy no matter where I slept or how cool it was at night. I assumed it had to be my reoccurring night terrors that brought on all the sweating.

I worked my butt off despite the harsh working conditions, but by the time September hit, the loopy feeling was taking its toll and I had to give my notice. Aside from giving myself a few days' break before heading off to the University of Washington, something had been gnawing at me—hinting at me, telling me that it's time to tell Mother the secret I hadn't been able to.

EIGHTEEN

SUFFOCATING SPITE

CAN I JUST pretend that today didn't happen? *So . . . why did I think that telling her would be such a good idea?* It's hard to get her yelling, ". . . dare you . . . talk . . . your Scoutmaster . . . " out of my mind. I tried convincing myself it didn't hurt . . . but it did just as much good as trying to convince myself that Bruce's damage didn't either.

I am so drained. Today just wiped me out.

Praying before I went to bed, I asked God why I had been so betrayed—by everyone, it seemed. Reaching for my Bible, I skimmed through the delicate pages one by one. My eyes fell on Matthew 6:14: "For if you forgive other people when they sin against you, your heavenly Father will also forgive you."

Really, God?

Forgiving was the last thing I wanted to do. I wanted my bitterness vindicated, my revenge approved, and God to punish my mother and Bruce.

And then . . . there it was, "But if you do not forgive others their sins, your Father will not forgive your sins."

God was speaking straight to my arrogance, loud and clear. My eyes filled with tears as I begged for Him to forgive me.

My heart was hurting. My eyes were heavy. With my Bible still open and resting on my chest, I dozed off to sleep from pure exhaustion. I probably needed to be that exhausted to sleep that well.

I woke to the sun shining through my curtains. More than ready to jump ship, I got up, made my bed, and gathered all I had ready to take with me and piled it all up by the bedroom door. My packed suitcase, my duffel, and all my comfort mechanisms to ensure that I would be set to rest my head elsewhere. I'd make it work wherever I slept—I was determined to not come back home.

I was shocked to smell the makings of breakfast cooking. Mother had unexpectedly fixed my favorite meal of scrambled eggs with cheese. I ate quickly in between Dad's small talk to avoid the likelihood of an argument with Mother. I wanted to avoid sitting at the same table altogether, but I could never resist food. Excusing myself from the table, I rinsed and placed my dishes in the sink, and said a simple, "Thanks."

Down the hallway and back to my room, I realized, *I'm really getting out of here. Way too much history attached to my life here.*

"Ready, Son?" Dad asked.

Eagerly, I replied with an enthusiastic, "Yes."

Dad grabbed my suitcase. I grabbed my duffel bag. Juggling everything else, I turned around to grab on to the doorknob, and then shut the door on what I couldn't change.

With the trunk of the Dodge Aspen all loaded up, I scrunched in the backseat, belted in the middle, giving me ample legroom on each side. I had run out of time to say goodbye to Virgil. More than likely, I had purposely dodged my chance, thinking it would have been way too emotional for both of us.

I could see Dad's face in the rearview mirror, looking as if he was in deep thought. I looked over to see what kind of look Mother had on her face, but she was not in my view. When we got down to the bottom of the road and passed Bruce's parents' house, I deliberately looked away. I sure didn't want a whiff of that man clinging to me.

Him coming to say good-bye to me the day before was bad enough.

With Dad's opera music resounding from the speakers, I thought, *I shouldn't have told Mother about Bruce at all.*

Her rejection had twisted my heart and wouldn't let go. I knew for my own sake that I needed to leave her denial behind just as I had to do with Bruce's damage.

Arriving at the campus, it was a welcome reprieve, as not much was said the entire car ride. I got out and walked back to the trunk where Dad helped me fetch my belongings. As we walked down the corridor, Mom started in on her usual, "Remember to . . ." and "Don't forget to . . ."

I humored her all the way down the hall with my, "Yes, Mother," on each point she stressed. At the end of the hall, we found my room on the right. Room 127.

Inside, Dad quickly put down the suitcase, appearing to be too antsy to stay. He told Mom that he'd be waiting for her in the car.

I had never seen him cry, and that day was no exception. He proceeded with his usual man-to-man good-bye to me, and his routine, "Love you," then left me alone with Mother.

It was just Betty Lou and me, and the strange feeling between us.

She stepped a few side steps over to be face-to-face in front of me. Grabbing both of my hands in each one of hers, she looked up into my eyes. Experience told me to guard myself against any words she might slam me with.

If anything, I knew it would have been a waste of time to hope for some miraculous apology for not believing me, so I just waited.

Surprisingly, tears started streaming down her face. That made my own tears flow. When she began sobbing, my resentment traveled toward understanding. The many years of what I perceived as criticism from her was translated into, "I'm so proud of you my son; you did it."

My mouth dried up too much to say anything back to her, but the tears said all that she needed. We wept together. This was the first time I had ever felt she actually had loved me. I hugged her tightly like a little boy needing his mommy. When I released my bear hug, it released eighteen years of suffocating spite I had in me. I grabbed her hands again and said, "Thank you Mother, thank you."

Wiping my tears, I realized the tight knots in my stomach had been loosed, and any animosity against my mom had been erased.

College was a little overwhelming at first, but I was prepared for that. Mom conditioned me that way. Some trickling of what her *kick-in-the-butt* influence did for me was humbling me, and I had to shamefully admit, *she was right*.

A chemical engineering degree was where I was headed. No other career fit my personality better. My already disciplined study habits, drive, and Mother's demanding training helped me buckle down and achieve honors' status that first quarter.

I adjusted quite well. I had to. Unless I wanted to go back home, and, that wasn't going to happen. Even though I was away from Mother, keeping her control at length was not as easy as I thought it would be. What a nut I was to think that it all went back home the day my parents dropped me off. From her perfection perch at the kitchen table, she was going to make sure my viola was not going to collect any dust. She shoved the sign-up form for the symphony in front of me. To please her, well . . . to hush her, I tried out. Her pressing in for me to acquire a seat in the proclaimed University of Washington Symphony did not get her the results she was used to. With me as the only nonmusic major, I ended up as last chair . . . meaning, the worst of the best. Betty Lou Stewart had never experienced me being the worst at anything.

I'm glad Mother's mood prepared me for all the privileged attitudes. I wasn't going to even risk asking out any of the girls. Dad already warned me about not getting caught up with someone like Mom, and some seemed too much like her. There were plenty other options around campus, so I resorted to our weekly dorm dances. Never having a date, I always went stag with the other honor students. The top 25 from around the country. The same type of band geeks and smart nerds I clicked with since grade school. It just felt comfortable being one of the nerdiest amongst the nerdiest. So, the dorm dances became our social event of the week. We geeks huddled together and competed to be the first to get a girl to dance. We either got a pass or a fail. If one in the bunch got lucky enough to slow dance with a girl, he passed with honors. I made sure to position myself as the perfect slow dance catch. It reminded me of my competitiveness in sports. I was determined to be an all-star ladies' man.

NINETEEN

X-RAY

WHILE MY STUDIES were going well, my sleep routine was not. Out of my element and away from home, more tragic nightmares resurfaced, screaming at me to deal with. So many triggers reminded me of Bruce's gun in my face ready to fire off. Fireworks sparked the image of gunfire. A backfiring vehicle made my body flinch at the boom.

Near the end of fall quarter, right before Christmas break, I was wrestling with my friend Kent in my dorm room. It got out of hand, and I went flying over him to where my chest hit the edge of the bedpost. I hit so hard, it felt like I blew the air out of my lungs. I didn't want to cry, but couldn't help it; the pain was intense. Slumped over, I climbed on my bed to try and get comfortable. It was tolerable as long as I stayed in a curled-up position. I told Kent that I would go and get it checked out the next morning at the campus health clinic. *I must have broken a rib or something.* The x-ray didn't show any fractures, but it did show something that concerned the doctor there. A dark haze was hovering near my heart and lung. He informed me, "It is imperative, Tom, you make an appointment, and go see your doctor right away."

Mom called for me. They had an opening the following week. It worked out perfectly since I would be on Christmas break.

On the bad side, Dad happened to lose his job at American Plywood Association. On the good side, it allowed him to be there with me. I was happy about that.

First, the doctor called for a MRI. The grim look on his face told us the results. I was quickly scheduled for a biopsy. The pit of my stomach knew what that word might mean.

Those days of waiting were the longest days of patience I was ever forced to wait.

"It's Hodgkin's Lymphoma," the doctor said.

While I was on the cusp of hyperventilating, Mom's frantic bellowing drowned out what the doctor was trying to say. I held my head in my hands, feeling the full weight of the diagnosis. I could do nothing else but pray, *How do I get through this, Lord?*

It was difficult to hear myself praying over the sounds of Mother's crying. Her tears had soaked her now torn-to-shreds tissue.

The doctor started to explain my options for treatment, but I wasn't listening—until his voice lightened up, "You're lucky, Thomas, as it was caught early; in stage one. The probability of remission is very high." He added, "If you had been diagnosed any later, it most likely would have been fatal."

I looked upward to mouth, *Thank you, Lord.*

In the car on the way home, I was feeling an undeniable peace. I had felt fragments of God's presence before, but never had it registered as powerfully as it did driving down that road.

I stayed home through Christmas break, and used the time as a complete sabbatical to make sense of what was ahead of me. I revved up my prayers, *Okay, Lord, I am now still enough to hear you. I am milled down to nothing, I'm waiting for what you want me to do through this. In Jesus' name, amen.*

Going back to college after break, my heaviest of burdens remained back at home. My mother. She seemed to be severely depressed with the news of my cancer. I tried to reassure her I was in the best place possible for treatment, living right there on campus. Her emotions were ragged. She leaned on me for support through her repetitive phone calls. She'd sigh helplessly, and whimper, "I can't even get myself out of bed, Tom. The stress is too much for me to bear."

I didn't have the heart to remind her that it was me who was starting radiation treatments, and it was me who had the cancer.

I'd patiently listen on my end of the receiver—as long as it took to pacify her worries. That's one thing she taught me as her son . . . an infinite amount of patience.

Her phone calls were getting harder to take. The initial shock of my diagnosis had worn off, and some bad feelings were emerging. I was glad she couldn't see the annoyed expression on my face.

It all rapidly accelerated into downright disappointment. I couldn't figure out why she was so devastated over my cancer, but the horrible abuse from Bruce could be dismissed like it was nothing? It was hard, but I was determined to resist acting out any disrespect towards her. A confrontation like that would have been a bigger battle than fighting off my cancer.

I exhaled to decompress from our irritating conversation. The distance between us is what's keeping me sane.

Sliding my journal out from the nightstand, I opened it on my bed and flattened out the seam so I could write. In black pen, I spelled out the word CANCER in all capital letters at the top of the fresh page. No matter how you say it, that word is scary, so I thought it best to start off with, *Okay, Lord, please take it from here.*

As verbatim as possible, I scribbled down everything that was coming to me, ". . . you were meant to be assigned that dorm room . . . you were meant to wrestle that night . . . you were meant to hurt your rib."

I stopped writing as it was sinking in . . . *Oh my goodness, I get it.*

I continued to write all the way down to the bottom of the page, until it ran over to the next page.

The doctor's words were saved for the entire next page.

This could be my own personal miracle in the making. How could it not?

I wrapped up my revelation writing this note, "*I'm leaning on you, Lord. I'm letting my faith rise above my fear.*"

TWENTY

HAPHAZARD

IF ANYONE'S CHILDHOOD could have prepared someone for something as trying as cancer, it was mine. I was determined to take a step at a time, and march ahead to whatever it took to beat this disease.

Cat scans located exactly where the cancer was attacking me. Pinpointed with small marks etched into my chest, a dotted map was tattooed front and back to aim the radiation. It was definitely not the kind of tattoo I imagined I would get.

Radiation treatments lasted for over three months. I am not sure what was worse—the radiation causing constant nausea and puking, or the painful tests and treatments. I cringed when the dull, three-inch needles were inserted into my chest, and tubes were implanted in the tops of my feet.

I tried not to concentrate on the agony during the procedures. Instead, I focused an intense curiosity on what was taking place.

Of course, my engineer mind was in the ideal setting.

I analyzed the process of the tubes used to infiltrate dye into my lymph node system through my veins. My goal of wanting to be a chemical engineer had been confirmed after watching all of that.

Feeling so tired and sick most days, I had to emotionally and physically force myself to get up and drag myself out of bed. I knew I could have so easily fallen into a martyr complex, so I reminded myself,

Others are going through this too. If this was another sacrifice I had to endure, so be it.

Remarkably, through it all—I don't know how—other than with God's help—I maintained my 4.0 grade average.

On alternating nights, I would intensely study, leaving maybe five hours to squeeze in some sleep. The next day, staying alert and awake in class was almost impossible. Then the next night, I'd need at least ten full hours of sleep to rejuvenate enough to function. Missing class was not an option.

Quitting school momentarily crossed my mind. Then I came back to common sense and reminded myself, *There is no way I want to go back home and live with Betty Lou again.*

Jokes about me gradually began to filter through campus. The punchline had my name all over it. Why was it so funny about my hair being stuck in the shower drains? It wasn't funny to me.

I just wanted to say, *Come on people, grow up.*

I learned very quickly that the bullying I had already endured my entire life hadn't yet ended. The guys laughed and pointed at me like it was my pubic hair left behind. I couldn't believe the cruelty, even knowing I was fighting cancer.

With my treatments scheduled in the mornings, I could make my classes in the afternoon. Often, I'd feel nauseous in the middle of class, and stop to vomit in chemistry lab.

In the middle of all the negatives, my concern was growing deeper for other cancer patients like me. We could share in each other's battle, and console any sadness we had.

Going to treatment is what I dreaded. Not the radiation itself, but to find out that another patient I knew had died since I had last seen them.

I had never experienced such grief before. My parents' less-than-genuine emotions had always felt so artificial. It was a brand-new adventure for me to experience this raw emotion for myself, but I surely wasn't expecting to receive it in such a powerful dose all at once.

Along with the families who lost their loved ones, and the doctors who lost their patients, I was overcome with emotions of sorrow, confusion, and sometimes anger when I lost my new friends too. Even though negative emotions may have skewed my focus at times, God quickly reminded me to refocus back towards Him by using the circumstances as an open opportunity to spread His word into their pain. I did just that. I'd recite scriptures that were helping me to share what comforted me. Psalm 147:3 was one of my favorites. "He heals the brokenhearted and binds up their wounds." In the midst of it all, by embracing others, I sensed God's purpose for me. After all that I had gone through with Bruce and came out on the other side, I knew God could do it again with cancer.

Dad phoned me late on a Sunday night after I had fallen asleep. Still half asleep, I scrambled for the phone. Dad seemed hyped up as he started talking fast about an article he ran across in the newspaper. I could hear Mom muttering some not-so-kind words in the background. His angst seemed to accelerate with each word. I listened to his shaky voice as he streamed out disturbing facts from what he was reading, "People working in factory-type setting are being exposed to cancer-causing toxins without their knowledge." Of course, he was referring to the chemical plant I had worked at last summer. His voice got gruffer when he said some employers were aware of these conditions, but chose to be haphazard about the safety of their workforce. He talked about companies who also neglect to caution their employees about the potential dangers of carcinogen exposure.

Understandably, Dad was mad. Mother was even more furious.

At the end of the article, he paused for my reaction. I was definitely wide awake, as I came to grips with where my cancer may have come from.

Before I could respond, Dad shouted out what he was going to do. "If it wasn't so late, I'd be speeding over to my attorney's office."

I could hear my mother was in her nonstop tyrant mode. She squawked behind Dad, "No one will ever put a Stewart in harm's way and get away with it. That damned chemical plant." She was so loud, I'm glad it was muffled a bit by Dad on the phone in between us. Poor Dad, she was blaming him, "Damn you, Bob, you got him the job there."

Dad couldn't muster up any rebuttal.

Their squabbling left me feeling squeamish, just as it always did. While the brunt of what Dad had just dropped on me settled in, I waited for him to collect himself, hoping Mom would shut up for once and stop interrupting. Thankfully, her hollering tapered down when Dad sternly told her, "Go to the bedroom and calm down for a while." I was surprised that she actually did.

Good for you, Dad, I thought, *you're finally standing up to her.* I hoped she wouldn't take it out on him after we hung up the phone.

With a heavy sigh, he told me, "We are going to make this right, and go after the plant."

I waited for him to finish before saying, "It's in God's hands, Dad, not ours. Vengeance is His."

I knew the reason Dad wanted to pursue legal action. His motivation, the same as Mother's, was always for personal gain. In other words, it was the Stewart way. All I wanted to do was to be free of this evil demon that had staked its claim upon me.

Nevertheless, there was nothing I could do to stop Dad's push or Mom's pull. Those two stubborn Stewarts would insert themselves to get what they wanted, with no regard to anyone in their path. Whether it was Dad's greed or whatever Mom's issue was, God would do what He wanted with this, His way.

I was completely relying on that to heal me the same . . . His way. That would've been retribution enough for me. Going to court and suing the chemical plant would not heal me. But then maybe, just maybe, blowing the whistle on the lax safety hazards of this company might prevent someone else from contracting Hodgkin's the way I did.

Out of curiosity, I asked Dad to read the toxins listed in the article. I really wished that I hadn't. He rambled down the list until he came to the last one. It was naphtha. *Ah, now I get why Mother was so mad.* It wasn't about the chemical plant at all. It was about how that toxic soap ended up in my mouth by her hand.

I flinched, and had to hang up before she shifted the blame towards me.

Just as I thought, her guilt spikes her temper. Thrusting herself into tirades is her way of deflecting her faults. *No wonder I ran to Bruce.*

My mood was not going to fester in what used to be. I wasn't going to drift into finding fault. After my firsthand exposure to so much death in the cancer wing, where coping with heartbreak is the norm, everything else seemed petty in comparison. As it was, three other close friends of mine had also been diagnosed with Hodgkin's, like me. None of them worked at the same plant as I did, but I was curious as to what they might have been exposed to along the way. One passed away, one was on the brink of no hope, and the other was not taking it seriously, and refused to listen to me.

I knew I needed to immerse myself in my studies while continuing to pray for that miracle. Best to let Mom and Dad do what they are going to do and stay out of their way. I knew Dad needed a purpose after losing his job. And, well, Mom needed a purpose to prove she was right. I just hoped they'd exhaust themselves before they do anything rash and expect me to join them in on their trek of revenge.

I was really proud of Dad, though. For once, he did not allow Mother's force to stunt his motivation. It felt invigorating to witness, but it was short-lived. Dad's plan of action was interrupted midstream when my blood sample analysis came back with nothing definitive. There was no pentachlorophenol detected. If there had been, it would have been proof enough for legal action. Traces must have been diminished by the radiation. For me, this was a relief. I didn't want to be a part of their scheme in the first place.

I was getting strange vibes from Mom and Dad. They actually seemed disappointed. It appeared that the dollar signs they banked on had caught their attention more than I ever had.

I had just hit the three-month mark of my treatments.

Acknowledging the soft knock on the door of the exam room, the doctor came in, holding my chart. Sitting next to my parents, he brushed by and took his spot on the rollaway stool in front of me.

I felt like an impatient child in grade school anxious for show-and-tell. With a slight grin, he opened the front cover of my file and said, "Well, it looks like the Man upstairs has many more important tasks for you in this world, Tom."

All my words were stuck in my throat just like when I first found out the bad news. The doctor continued, "No chemotherapy necessary, Tom." Usually, my emotions were so programmed to link with Mother's, my normal first reaction was to look to her for what I was supposed to feel. This time, I immediately looked straight up.

Goose bumps raised on my arms as my blubbering cry took over. The doctor added one more wonder to my miracle. "Being able to have children someday, Tom, should not be an issue. Your reproductive organs were spared."

More than relieved, I stood up. The doctor and I exchanged wide smiles. I hugged him as tight as I could, squeezing my sincere thanks.

TWENTY-ONE

ZERO

TINGLES OF EXHILARATION ran through my body as I sang praises to God in the front row of church. With my own out-of-tune melody, I piped out, "Amazing Grace." Thankfully, I was drowned out by the piano, but God heard me; He didn't care what I sounded like.

The church body prayed over me that day. As I knelt down, they surrounded me and thanked the Lord for His favor on me. The hands resting on my shoulders guided me all the way down to the floor into what I was ready for . . . absolute submission. As they prayed, I murmured my own prayer, "You cleansed me of cancer, Lord, and you cleansed me of Bruce. Thank you for carrying me through the darkness. In Jesus' name, amen."

Junior year, I started off just where my intentions wanted to go. My cancer fight hadn't held me back—I had been accepted into University of Washington's Chemical Engineering School.

Moving out of the dorm into the fraternity interrupted my nighttime routine again, and stirred up my unpredictable sleep patterns.

155

Finally free from cancer, I couldn't wait to start feeling like a semi-normal dude, but mostly, looking forward to getting on with my life. Well, I would try anyway. Time may have passed since Bruce, but he was still alive and well in the middle of the night. During the day, I did everything I could to keep him hidden. Trying to stay above what was really going on with me, I would try and fit in. Inappropriate humor was a crutch I used to seek attention. Oh, I got the attention all right; thinking I was funny. I was the only one who thought I was. I wasn't, and it backfired. The insulting sarcasm ran off any girl who may have wanted to spend time with me.

I heard that living the famed frat life was a sure bet to hook up with a female, and thought this Stewart could just merge into the scene . . . just like that. *Here's my chance,* or so I thought.

It didn't take me long to realize I really needed to tone down my weirdness and my cocky side to even come close to mingling with the opposite sex. Fitting the mold of the fraternity type-of-cool was not in my makeup. I still hadn't drunk a drop of anything alcoholic, and smoking was definitely out of the question. I knew there were more carcinogens in cigarettes than in the toxic chemicals that caused my cancer. No amount of peer pressure would breach this boy's clean slate.

Nevertheless, with my need for approval skyrocketing, I continually sought out the admiration of others. The hereditary Stewart pride was becoming a dominant trait in me the older I got. My commitment to and active involvement with Campus Crusade for Christ helped me through the typical college temptations, but those were not my issues. My out-of-control lusting issues were. Frat life seemed to be measured by as much association as possible with women. Living my life with them didn't make it any easier; it enhanced it. Battles between my physical desires and my spiritual convictions continued, battling even more with my conscience, telling me that Bruce changed me completely as a man and I might never change back.

I'd stand in the background behind the cool guys observing. I think my yearning for the girls to swarm around me was pathetically obvious. I was on a constant freeway, having to prove to myself that Bruce hadn't stolen my charisma. Or, maybe I never had any in the first place. My braces, zits, and glasses were gone long ago in the past, so that wasn't it. *What was it about me?* It's as if the girls sensed what had happened to me and did whatever they could to steer clear from the aroma that Bruce left behind still stuck on me.

Surrounded by so many beautiful girls prancing around at all hours didn't lessen my desires. My greatest weakness was watching them moseying right in front of me; half naked in their skimpy bikinis, passing by this lonely geek. *Now that I'm cancer free, maybe they will be attracted to me now?* I'd daydream about a harem of hotties flocking around me to fill my every desire, but I knew that would only happen to me behind the lids of my shut eyes.

Who am I fooling? What babe would want this violated piece of Bruce-meat anyway? I'm a pitiful, last-boy-standing loser. I'll just hunker down and bury myself in my books. I'm good at that.

But I was having some difficulties focusing. Not that the content was more challenging than any of the other prerequisites I had aced, but for some reason, I couldn't think clearly. It was as if my brain was on lockdown. I knew if I were still fighting cancer, there would have been no way I could have gone on like this.

December rolled around and it was time for my quarter final. My confidence went in ahead of me and reality followed. I blew it! I blanked! Sitting in my chair, I stared at the test on my desk with no idea how to answer the questions. Going from an A student straight to a zero on an exam was not going to go over well with Mother. *What's wrong with me?* Something had to be wrong. That wouldn't have mattered to Mother. *When she finds out, she is going to make something wrong with me.* My deepest gut worry had always been doing poorly in anything.

I was right. My first failure was just as horrible as I had agonized about. Mother was hellish. She accused me of conforming to the sinful frat lifestyle, and blamed me for downright carelessness. In her eyes, this was pure disrespect against her every expectation for me to succeed. She made sure to rub in how it was an unforgivable insult. "My next move,

Thomas Gregory Stewart, will be to rip you out and away from that peer pressure if you don't improve," she threatened.

I had to find out the reason, even just to get some relief from her. Fueled by her threats, I headed straight to the doctor's office where I relayed all the strange symptoms. I thought I was done with the prodding of needles, but it was necessary to see what was wrong.

"Your thyroid is dangerously low, Tom. I'm glad you came in when you did. This could have been fatal."

Speechless, I wondered, *Why me?* This was the second time I had been told I could have died.

Further tests concluded the radiation treatments had scattered to my thyroid and killed it off, but my vital organs had all been protected. Once prescribed medication, my ability to function gradually returned. With or without mother's behavior, getting that zero on my final didn't sit well with me at all.

Watching Betty Lou Stewart humbled firsthand was a sight to see. With the undeniable truth about my thyroid, Mother sucked up the fact that her accusations had no relationship to my zero score and instantly zipped her mouth. She had nothing more to say to me.

My trials seemed to be breaking down the pride of my parents. I'll admit I was happy to see a small glimmer of humility being cultivated in the sacred walls of the Stewart pride.

After my first-ever fail, I tried not to beat myself up too much, but that one final grade had derailed me off my degree track. Almost on my knees in the office of my mentor, the chairman of the Chemical Engineering Department, I begged for some consideration. When he said, "Maybe you should go home until winter quarter starts," I think he could see the desperation in my eyes, and felt sorry for me.

I gulped so loudly, I'm sure he heard it. My voice cracking, I asked, "Sir, with all due respect, may I please ask what my other options are?"

With a smile, he asked me in an understanding tone, "Would it happen to be your mother?"

I exhaled about as empty as my lungs could go. I felt he agreed with me, but had to abstain out of political correctness. He said quietly, "Tom, I have received an overabundance of phone calls from her, inquiring about your performance . . . so many that I have memorized her phone number, and now conveniently do not answer."

We both couldn't help but laugh.

Then he said, "Tom, this is what we are going to do. Since your classes are not available until winter, you may attend the same classes you would have. You'll be what is referred to as auditing. The same as an observer. No credits will be granted, but it will benefit you tremendously when you do legitimately take the classes. There will be no tests given to you, and no homework due; therefore, no studying. A freebie of sorts."

I could have kissed his shoes, as my anxiety about going home vanished completely.

For the very first time ever, having my academic plate nearly empty, I had to practice filling up spare time. I never had any before. Still dragging around my wounds from Betty Lou and Bruce made me feel normalcy was always just out of arms' reach. I felt incredibly lonely. Being single on a Friday night with nothing else to do, I headed back to my dorm stomping grounds to meet up with the old group of my outcast buddies—the ones who made it fun to be a drip.

I tagged along with them back to the weekly dorm dances where I felt comfortable. Walking in, rehearsing my best pick-up lines, my Stewart swagger must have risen above the competition. Only five minutes into the dance, I scored an A+ when I connected to eyes scouting me from across the dimly lit room. A beautiful girl—with curly, long blonde hair she had swept behind her ears—moved confidently toward me. It was too dark to see the color of her eyes through her glasses. She was about a foot shorter than me, graced with an adorable smile. I was attracted to her immediately, and; best of all, I didn't feel like such a nerd anymore. I just felt really tall.

She grabbed my hand and pulled me to the middle of the dance floor. We stopped just under the shine of the twirling disco ball, in between the flashes of the bright strobe lights. That's where I noticed her adorable freckles.

I would have preferred if the DJ had played a slow dance instead of a fast tempo so my clumsiness wouldn't embarrass her, but I was actually proud of myself when my body actually grooved to the beat. When the song came to an end, the lights brightened enough to shine on her face. She had blue eyes. *I love blue eyes.* Between our huffing and puffing to catch our breath, she was the first to introduce herself, "My name is Amy. Yours is Tom, right?"

I was surprised she knew my name—especially a female someone. I felt it was a God thing that we met, and I was also a little impressed with myself for catching the eye of an attractive and smart freshman. The instrumental start of the next song made my pulse beat harder. The party lights were dimmed down to match the mood of the ballad. If there ever was a song meant to work as the perfect, romantic tactic for a guy, it was "Open Arms" by Journey.

With the height difference between us, I was hoping she wouldn't get a crick in her neck from having to look up at me. Yet, the sparkle of romance in her eyes showed she didn't mind. In a smooth ballet-type move, she raised herself up on her tiptoes, and set us in motion by draping her arms around my neck and nestling in.

Chills rushed up and down my body, totally new sensations for me. I didn't know this could feel so good. Before, arousal had tied me to the disgust of Bruce. *Not anymore!* I told myself, *don't mess this one up, Tom. Don't scare her away. Don't say anything stupid.*

I could feel her hold on me loosen from around my neck. She pulled back and looked at me, then didn't waste any time before she leaned in and up and kissed my mouth. I never had a girl go in for the kiss first before. Our mutual, easy laughter shattered the rest of the ice that needed to be broken.

Amy's forwardness was refreshing.

I was more than relieved with our immediate connection on the dance floor. Our slow dance together felt so natural, the way it should be between a guy and a girl. Maybe I didn't need to worry about my confused testosterone.

The applause I received from my audience of guy pals up against the wall added to my confidence.

As we danced, my thoughts raced. *I sure hope Amy knows what she is getting into.* I knew that I'd better warn the next woman who gave me any attention at all that I would be hanging on pretty tight. Countless girls had accepted my awkward invitations for a date, but then had rapidly made their getaways after the first date. It had to be my quirky mannerisms that scared them away.

I hadn't had a chance to warn those girls of what they were in for. I knew any girl who spent time with me would have to compensate for the love and nurturing I never had.

But Amy was different. Very different. Like me. It was her forward, first-move approach that made me believe right away—*she's the one!*

TWENTY-TWO

MANHOOD

OUR INTELLECTS BECAME the basis of our relationship. That was what we had in common—and I used it as my cover. I was buying time for the inevitable, stalling for the next stage Amy was broadly hinting about. I couldn't bear the thought of her fleeing like the others, but the thought of not waiting until marriage to have sex bothered me just the same. It was my sex drive that could care less about my convictions.

She admitted she was not a virgin. I didn't care either way. The dilemma I was struggling with was whether or not I still was.

My convictions were keeping me strong for the time being, but I felt as if my willpower to do right was being drained. Then I worried about when the time did come to be intimate, Bruce's damage would affect every part of me. I knew as a Christian I shouldn't even go there, but not knowing if I was even able to perform as a man haunted me even more.

I really loved Amy. From the first night that I met her, I wanted to marry her. But thinking about marriage also brought up the abuse in me. Marriage equaled sex and Bruce equaled sex. I was having trouble separating the two. I constantly beat myself up how I wasn't a normal guy. Somehow; some way, I knew I had to sever the gross sex connection Bruce had enslaved me with, but how to do that without actually having intercourse, I didn't know.

Inevitably, it was time for Amy to meet Betty Lou. I really had to give Amy the rundown before she did.

Mother's not-so-welcome-home halted at the Shasta trailer parked in the orchard next to the house. Nothing had changed since Bruce's day. He still had been the only one invited into our home. That was okay; there was no way I would have wanted Amy to experience the embarrassing stash of accumulated stuff she'd see inside.

Mother looked Amy up and down, evaluating her. After finding out she was Norwegian like us, she was finally approved enough to enter the family's sacred abode on wheels. Inside the trailer, Mother had laid out her fine china. I could have guessed what Mother was going to try to impress Amy with. Fortunately, Amy wasn't a picky eater so spared herself the penalty of stepping on Mother's toes. Arranged so perfectly was Mom's idea of elegant—Norwegian goat cheese on crackers, with a side of liverwurst. I was kind of hoping the liverwurst would not be on the menu. Stinky stuff was not what I had in mind for what I had planned on for our date.

I impatiently waited for Mother to make her exit. We said grace after she was gone. At my "In Jesus' name, amen," Amy looked up at me from across the wobbly table. Her look reminded me of how our eyes met that first night.

We didn't even think about touching the food laid out before us.

My plan was that I would be positioned down on my knees in front of her by now, but my hands holding both of hers was even better. I had rehearsed my lines many times, but had to pause enough to make sure to tone down the desperation in my voice. Rubbing her fingers with my thumbs, I sat up straight and began, "Amy, I love you." Her eyes stopped me when they welled up. Her tears were more touching and poignant than any answer to a proposal I could have imagined. I gently eased my right hand away from hers, and slipped it down to retrieve the ring I had hidden under the seat cushion next to me. As I rummaged for it, it slipped off the seat and bounced with a very faint clang onto the vinyl floor. That move was not in my master plan.

As charismatically as I could, I eased out my side of the table to retrieve the diamond ring that sparkled up at me. Pivoting on my knee, I made it look as if that is what I meant to do in the first place.

Amy reached out her left hand, and posed her ring finger toward me, all the time weeping her answer of "Yes." She grabbed ahold of my shaky hand to help slide it on her finger. The moment was intense. About as romantic as it could get. She guided me by my elbow to stand up with her. We hugged each other tightly, but so tenderly. My heart soared. I never thought any girl would want to be with me, let alone marry me.

Taking charge, Amy held my hand, and stepped across the floor to flip down the lever on the door into the locked position. I was so moved by her response to my proposal, my body melted, and I just followed her lead. But an anxious thought intruded: *I wonder where Mother is.* She was probably watching from the house with her binoculars. I was thankful the curtains were already drawn in the trailer; otherwise, my imagination had her already pounding on the door.

"Are you prepared?" Amy asked.

Her question took me back to my visit to the drugstore down the street. I was scared to death to be spotted by anyone who might have known me. Embarrassment for this Stewart wasn't the case. It was the slight chance that Betty Lou might find out. A lecture like that would've lasted for days.

I slyly purchased my "sin-before-marriage" precautions, and dashed out the backdoor with the brown paper sack under my arm.

What I really wanted to tell her was, "I am an Eagle Scout. Since our Scout Motto just happens to be 'Be Prepared' . . . Of course, Amy. Yes, I am prepared."

But adding my dry humor to the moment would not have been the wisest of choices. So, I stuck with, "Yes, I am prepared."

Really, I was terrified. I knew I couldn't pray about any of this as we weren't yet married, but I knew it was going to happen. This is not how it is supposed to be. But my urges were taking over. It felt like the entire experience was corrupt long before we even started.

I am such an idiot. Amy must have been wondering why I wasn't opening my eyes to look at her. I couldn't. Behind my closed lids was a contaminated vision of Bruce's face peering behind me—instead of Amy's face in front of me. Deep inside I knew she needed to know how truly broken I was in that area before we took our vows and married. If it turned out my manhood was too messed up for her after we were married, that truly would not have been fair. In my engineer's way of reasoning, I tried to ease my way out of my guilt.

"Tom, look at me."

It took me a second, but I did. And . . . there she was! It was Amy's face I saw. Miraculously, the stain of what Bruce had done was no longer there. I felt like crying, but knew it was not the best time for tears in the position we were in.

The heaviest weight of my past was lifted off.

Bruce may have stolen my childhood, but heck if he stole my manhood!

But Amy's "Yes" was short-lived. It wasn't long before our plans were squashed. I don't know if Amy had cold feet, or if it was the stress of both of our mothers that did it.

There was nothing I could say to change her mind.

I was embarrassed and again felt like a loser. I was sure glad I held off on telling too many others about the engagement.

In a daze, feeling the sharp pain of being dumped, I stared down at the returned token of my love Amy dropped in the palm of my hand. As always, I shut off and walled off my feelings. I nestled the ring in my button-down shirt pocket, and walked my humbled pride over to a pizza parlor near campus with a sudden craving for a small olive, hamburger, and pineapple pizza.

I headed to sit in the middle of the corner booth. I was beyond sad, wanting to know, *Why is it me again who is the single guy sitting all alone? Gosh, I must have been mistaken, thinking I was finally a prize catch. Now I'm just sitting here like a prize fool.*

After my quick-fix pizza therapy was served to me, I placed a napkin on my lap and bowed my head as I usually did. Then came these words that entered my mind, *Tom, I've halted the hamster wheel you were on to make you stop long enough and be still.*

Startled, I glanced up and around the pizza place to see who might have been talking to me. It was empty. When I first walked in, I had been so focused on the need to fill my craving, I hadn't noticed that there were no other customers in the restaurant. There still weren't.

At any other time, the end to my prayers over my food gave me the ready-set-go-ahead to dig in. Not this time. My hands stayed cupped around my forehead, waiting to hear something else.

Although Bruce came into your life, he went. Your cancer came and went. Amy came and went. And, Betty Lou came and . . . well . . . she is your mother—just know, your suffering is not in vain.

Then there was quiet. I felt cradled in amazement as I embraced what were not my own thoughts. *I know it was you, Lord. I heard you loud and clear.*

With more peace than I had ever felt before, I walked out of the restaurant with a take-out box full of untouched, lukewarm pizza.

TWENTY-THREE

GOD'S ODDS

I PROMISED MYSELF I would not put myself into a position to fall again. It hurt too much to be dumped by what I thought could be a normal relationship. Maybe Amy had been just a deterrent to keep Bruce out of my mind. It worked for the short time I was with her, but now that she was gone, I struggled to keep my mind busy, so I plowed into my studies, determined to graduate at the top of my class. At least that would make me feel better.

My compartmentalized brain was prone to this. I considered it a gift so I could block out all the trauma in my life. It was a catch twenty-two though. Some of what was in my head would turn to a blur, and then I'd also forget the good stuff.

Miraculously, I had made it through Bruce. I made it through cancer. I was making it through heartbreak. All of this while making it through college, earning a Bachelor of Science degree in chemical engineering. *Lord, I couldn't have done it without you, thank you.*

I used my usual lay low and be quiet to just be still; giving my full attention to what God had planned for me next.

With that, more answered prayers started pouring in. A hiring door was unlocked and swung wide open to a chemical engineering position at the company I wanted.

The job was not the only answer to my countless prayers. God was showing me how my suffering was being redeemed, beginning with my cancer.

The primary responsibilities of my new job required me to research and implement safer alternatives for cleaning surfaces prior to painting. Chrome was present in the liquid immersion tanks used prior to the painting processes. The chrome solution had been deemed carcinogenic and employees were handling the toxins that may potentially cause cancer. *Who better to combat this issue but a person who had fought a cancer caused by the same chemicals?* My personal passion had been put into action. *Coincidence? Nope. God's odds!*

I was getting a feel of what God was telling me, and what He wanted me to understand in all of this (Genesis 50:20), "You intended to harm me, but God intended it for good to accomplish what is now being done, the saving of many lives."

Not by choice, I was living back with my parents until I could move to a place of my own. Mother made sure she took me back in time to my teenage years in the way she was treating me.

One night; instead of letting her get to me, I decided to hop in the car and go out and drive somewhere. It was raining, almost stormy. What I really needed was some place to walk off the stress Mother put on me. The only dry place I could think of was the mall. I don't care for the mall, but since it was pouring out, the mall it was.

Surrounded by all the shopping options I'm not interested in, I see her.

My feet come to a stop. I stand in front of the department store where she is working, blocking the steady flow of shoppers who detour around me.

All I can see is her back turned to me, but her beautiful, shoulder-length, brunette hair is what catches my eye.

The loneliness I hated with not having a woman in my life hinted how I couldn't pass her up. That alone gave me the push to walk over to the Men's Department where she was working. *I really don't need any jeans. Yet, if I'm going to meet her, I sure do.* I shuffled my feet to catch her attention. *That didn't work.* I make my way around her to the other side of the display where she was organizing. I notice that her name tag says, 'Ruth.'

Making sure I'm in plain sight, I rummage through the neatly stacked piles, pretending not to be able to find my size . . . even though I had already passed over three pairs that would fit me just fine.

I reenact my pitiful actions, until it must be obvious how helpless I really am. My adrenaline races into high gear, and my heart pounds when I hear the sweet sounds of, "Do you need any help, Sir?"

I wanted to kick myself when I forgot what pick-up line I was going to use.

Gracefully, the young woman reaches over and gives a sideways smile when she immediately finds my size I told her I needed. *She must be flattered by my charm.*

Looking at her name tag again, pretending I hadn't already, I stuttered, "Well, thank you very much, Ruth. You are truly something. May I call you Ruth?" *Oh shoot, I sound pathetic like my dad.*

Walking with her to the cash register, I tried to create a conversation about my new, prestigious position, hoping it would impress her. *It looks like it worked.* Her smile told me so.

I was so mesmerized by the way she handled herself, I tried to stall to be able to spend more time with her; hoping my compliments would snag her into giving me her phone number.

With the jeans that I didn't need in one hand, she handed me the sales receipt with her phone number jotted down on the back in the other. I winked at her to say thanks, and headed out the door.

I had never felt so fantastic. My washed-out ego had been rejuvenated. As I strolled out to my car, the rain had stopped. She was definitely a God thing. *Thank you, Lord.* Without a doubt, there was no way I could have taken one more day of feeling like a failure where women were concerned.

Back at home, Betty Lou seemed impatient, but excited, as she handed me an already opened, stamped envelope addressed to the Stewart family. As I opened the flap of the fancy envelope inside of the other, she could barely contain herself as I started to read. My head felt light and I had to sit down, noticing that it was an invitation from Bruce. *I wasn't prepared for this today.*

Faking a pleased reaction, I read the wedding announcement. Bruce was getting married. Confused, I held back from yelling out loud, *But I thought he was gay!* I already knew to keep my mouth shut, then always look to Mother for how I was supposed to react. No way was I going to risk trampling on her joy. Even if I had anything to say about it, she already put it on the calendar. Also, she had already planned on what we were all going to wear. My, "Yes, Mother," was best—whether I felt that way or not. Instead of having to agree with Mom about how wonderful Bruce's wedding would be, I humored her, "Yes, I'd like to go." My reason was not to see Bruce get married, it was my excuse to ask the cute girl I met to accompany me.

"Absolutely, you can bring a date," Mother said. She was very pleased. No matter how much anguish Bruce churned up within me, I knew I needed to be there. I needed to see for myself if watching him get married in the eyes of God would help me to be able to forgive him.

I dressed up in Mother's designated family attire, buttoning up the man side of me. I was going to show up in confidence, proving he hadn't ripped me apart completely.

With Ruth on my arm, and sitting by my side, the plan was to watch the ceremony from afar. To no avail, Mother dragged us all as close to the front row on the groom's side as possible. Typical of Mother to place herself in the wedding party limelight even if she wasn't related. There she was, waving to get Bruce's attention. A tension knot formed in my neck from straining not to look at him.

The same pain in my neck he'd always been.

No sooner had the new Mr. and Mrs. been announced and the receiving line had formed, when Mother popped up to scurry over and reserve her up-front position in line.

Thinking fast on how to approach him, I told myself to be bold. I'd introduce my date as naturally as possible, as if he had actually just been a normal Scout leader. I was so proud to have her accompany me as she helped me feel like the man I thought I had lost.

With the gap closing in, a rock was settling in the pit of my stomach; I knew I had to shake his hand. But, the closer we came to approaching him, my feelings of animosity were fading. My subconscious kicked me into the same old auto-mode routine, as if nothing wrong had ever happened. This had to be how I made it through all those years in the company of him.

Reaching out with my right hand, I waited for his hello by eye contact. *Didn't happen.* He looked down while giving me a loose handshake and swooped up to introduce his new wife. I must have had to see her in person to make myself believe she was real. For a quick second, I thought about spilling the beans, but of course, her wedding was not the place. *How could she not know?* She was quiet and pleasant. A nice, church-going, Christian woman. Maybe she was just the right person to help him. *God, please make it so.*

We were pushed to continue through the line, and shuffled down to the end where we introduced ourselves to who just happened to be the new stepchildren of Bruce. I gulped. A daughter and a son. *Oh, my gosh!* They were not little kids, they were older teenagers, but, so was I.

I don't even want to think about this. Do I warn them? Why would I? If my own mother didn't believe me, why would anyone else? Maybe his new wife really *didn't know?* I wouldn't think that any mother would knowingly take that risk. But then again, I am no one to talk with the kind of parents I had. Or even myself for that matter.

His gun stays stuck in the same place it always has been—in the front of my mind, as vibrant as it was on those days that he pointed it at me.

I worry that his wife and her children are in the same predicament, living in fear of Bruce's threatening trigger finger.

I couldn't look at him for the rest of the night. Ruth and I slipped out the backdoor so I didn't have to say good-bye.

Driving her home, I so wanted to tell her, but the thought of Bruce's gun kept my mouth sealed.

I never imagined how a first date could have been worse and then better all at the same time. I just hoped she had a good enough time with me to want a second one. The amazing kiss she planted on my lips told me what her answer was. Our connection had my mind wander to where it should not have gone with her yet; I couldn't help it. But then, as Bruce always did, visuals of him with his new wife invaded our goodnight kisses—thinking about his wedding night consummation with his new wife made me want to vomit. I felt sorry for her. *He must just reek with little boy virginity, including mine.*

I wasn't sure where my heart was at. The strange off-beating in my chest was all over the place. There was one thing that I knew for sure. I hadn't come any closer to forgiving Bruce. That was for sure.

With the recent scent of matrimony in the air, not much time passed by before I wanted Ruth to take my last name. Standing on my Stewart forwardness, I retrieved the rejected ring from my first proposal and readied it to take the risk.

I didn't want to look desperate, but I also didn't want her to come up with an excuse to run like my first fiancé did. So, it was time to spice up my Stewart charm that got her attention in the first place, and pop the question.

I was the happiest man on earth with her "Yes" to me. We married just a few months later on Valentine's Day.

I was on pins and needles until we got to the "I do" part, followed by our seal-the-deal kiss, breathing again when the pastor announced us as man and wife.

Unfortunately, after the excitement of the honeymoon period ended, it didn't take long before I had bounced right back into the same loneliness I had when I was single.

Withering away in a catatonic existence was not what I promised in our wedding vows. It all reminded me too much of my parents.

That all-too-familiar way of life I grew up with prompted a phone call to my Dad. I started to compliment him for staying with Mom for so long. He stopped me mid-sentence with a strange tone in his voice, "I am divorcing your mom."

It sure sounded like Dad had been planning his own midlife crisis for quite some time. Matt had moved out now too, and he had plans for his future that didn't include Mom, as to where he wanted to travel, and such.

I understood him. Having been smashed down nonstop for that long, I'm sure he wanted to see how it felt to feel good about himself for once before he got too old. I couldn't say I didn't understand. Matt and I were the lucky ones, we both got to move out. Overall, I do appreciate him sticking it out as long as he did until Matt and I were grown.

Throughout the long, grueling divorce proceedings, Mom's health deteriorated very quickly. I was her crutch, and she used me to the limit as her support system, and her taxi driver when she was no longer able to drive. She was so frail. The divorce took its toll on me, and her demands started to take their toll on my marriage. Finally, it all took its toll on her, and she finally passed away. Unbeknownst to me, she was also addicted to painkillers, and died at 68.

My mind was blank. I didn't know how to feel. *Do I cry? Do I sigh a sigh of relief? That sounds horrible. I don't know how to feel.*

Did I ever thank her for the good stuff she did? I'm so confused.

Her death was probably not the best time to evaluate my ill feelings. It seemed the cost I paid to be her son cultivated what came to be my unhealthy, strong desire to seek attention and approval in whatever way I could. I loved her; I did, but I had to admit that it was a bit freeing to detach from my role as her perfect puppet.

The grief I was supposed to be going through shut itself out like everything else. Besides, there was a bigger job at hand. Drudging and sorting through thirty years of Mom's hoarded debris that still cluttered the family home.

Cracking the front door open, I stepped inside. I peered around my childhood home. It was different. For the first time, the dread of Mother's badgering was not there. So much anger spewed out of her mouth, it must have been absorbed into the walls. In the silence, it was as if I could still hear it. Tension engulfed me. The feeling was as tangible as it was when I lived there, and I actually called out, "Is anyone here?" But the house was empty.

Alone, I took a last tour around the house, reminiscing room by room. I deliberately saved the basement for last. The eerie place where so much abuse had taken place. I hesitated before turning the doorknob, praying that God would rid me of what prevented me from seeing beyond my own pain. Especially now, with Mother gone, I wanted to be more thankful for what the good, the bad, and the ugly taught me—rather than what the bad and the ugly did to me.

With each step that I plunked down, the closer I got to the bottom, I felt a dense cold roll through me. I knew right away that the unnerving chill could no way be coming from anything good. The same chills that went through my body when Bruce did his thing with me were traveling back and forth throughout my veins.

"Lord, I beg you. Please make his presence leave this place. Please take these memories from me."

My prayer was interrupted when the hinges on the front door upstairs squeaked as it opened. Must be Dad and Matt. It was time to rid this basement of the bad and the ugly. Boldly, I stood up and firmly commanded any evil there to flee. "Satan, get out of my way and get out of this house." Leaving the rest up to God, I sprinted up the stairs, skipping every other one.

We all tried not to show our disgust; but couldn't resist the wisecracks, as we walked through Mother's stockpile left behind. Any formerly empty spaces were now chock full.

To sort through everything was a massive chore, but I'm glad we had that opportunity. Having a hoarder for a mother also meant that she kept every important thing about my life I had shut off. For what belonged to me, I sorted and boxed it all up to take home. *Thanks, Mom.* She gave me the chance to look back at my childhood through what lay in those boxes, without Bruce blocking my view.

When it was all said and done, it took two commercial-sized garbage Dumpsters, crammed full of more than 400 jumbo-sized, heavy-duty black garbage bags, to dispose of the rest of Mom's thirty-year hoarding addiction.

TWENTY-FOUR

THREE MIRACLES

WITH MOTHER IN heaven, I had to let go. She was a stronghold who kept me bound to hurts from my past. For so long, my psyche had been plagued by the deceitful lie burned into me by her that if I didn't excel or get an A+ in whatever I did, I was *not good enough*. My trials proved that wrong. I've learned that a passing grade was more than sufficient, as long as I showed up. I read that we are supposed to consider it pure joy when facing our trials. It is then that shows our character. I'm not quite to the pure joy part, but I am arriving at the understanding part.

It took the birth of my children to realize what pure joy was. The doctor proved himself correct when radiation did not affect my sperm. Three miracles—two boys and a girl! First, Brian, then Benny, and finally, my daughter Becca—the first Stewart girl in over a hundred years. I couldn't even describe the cheering going on in my head when they were born. Anticipation pounded in my chest as I saw a vision of my three future, basketball all-stars. I hoped they would be tall like me.

I prayed that they would do well in school and be awarded many college scholarships. What could make a dad prouder?

My three miracles showed me the first glimpse I ever had of unconditional love. They loved me—no matter what. I was their daddy. I found a new light in my life through them, as the light in my marriage was fading.

I couldn't quite put my finger on it, as I assumed children were supposed to enrich a marriage. It had me waiting for something glorious to happen . . . the "wedded bliss" I had heard so much about.

Constantly fearing the off-chance I might not have been able to have children at all; despite the doctor's hopes . . . when I did, I was overjoyed, and overindulged in my role of daddy. I sealed their days with a bedtime story, a hug, a kiss, and prayers each night. I wanted to be the kind of dad whose footsteps they would want to follow.

My most special Father's Day ever was when Brian and Benny gifted me with their handmade, big, black, oversized construction paper cards with their paint-stamped footprints they made at school. Their little feet dipped in bright white paint, starting at the bottom of the page—stepping down, one after another. Right, left, right, left, right, left, all the way to the top, ending with their tiptoes. These little white paper oval cutouts, snipped with those small child-safety scissors, pasted-on pencil written notes saying, "I want to follow in your footsteps." Both Father's Day cards have been tearstained with my love for them.

God gave me a purpose in my children. I think I was striving to be "Father of the Year." Not that anyone had to give me that title, I just wanted my kids to think I was. I knew the importance of teaching the commitment to do their best in school—without the intimidation level Mother imposed on me. I knew how much damage her tactics of humiliation caused.

Sports had indeed saved my life in many ways. Initially, it was to have an excuse to stay away from home . . . and, also keep my distance from

Bruce. Eventually, what was happening with me in my striving to claim some jock status was reversing some of the damage. My self-esteem was on its way to replenishing itself. I'm not quite sure if my nickname "Tom 'The Brain' Stewart" falls into the jock category, but I felt important just the same. I also wanted my kids to experience teamwork and sportsmanship, and build their own self-esteem. Their involvement in t-ball, baseball, soccer, basketball, flag football, and swimming did that. And, of course, no one could fill the shoes of coaching them but me.

Then the day came that Brian brought home the 'Join the Cub Scouts' flier from school. Benny was not old enough to join yet, but I included him as if he was. That sure took me back to the day I brought the same type of flier home to my dad. Brian had the same begging excitement I had, mimicked by his little brother standing right next to him. The same words that came out of my dad's mouth to me, came out of mine, "So, you want to join Cub Scouts?" I wanted my boys to feel as important as I did when my dad left a decision like that up to me.

As I pictured myself in the shoes of my boys standing there, I wanted to relay the same interest my dad did that day. My kids didn't know anything about Bruce, but I still wanted to pass on the valuable lessons he had taught me that he did do right.

Mother was now gone, and there was no one else who knew about the abuse I endured. *I had done okay with it as far as I could tell.* Or, so I thought. Seeing the innocence in my boys' eyes kept me bound to resentment for my dad not being there to protect me. I vowed to protect my sons by immersing myself in all activities they would be involved with while in Scouts . . . every step of the way.

I would be just as proud to wear the uniform of Scoutmaster, as I was the day way back when I had first joined up. Hanging on my every word, their eyes gleamed as they stood up taller when I stood up in front of them. I showed them the first step by saluting them with my fingers. In unison, they followed my lead. I told them, "It is my promise, boys, I will take you all the way to Eagle Scout."

TWENTY-FIVE

UNFOUNDED

MY DADDY BLISS is what drove me. As for that wedded bliss I was waiting for, dissolution papers are what drove me out of the house. After fifteen years of marriage, Ruth took me by complete surprise. She tried to reason with me, as if I was supposed to understand, "We are going in different directions." I wasn't quite sure which direction she meant by that.

I had to stop and really evaluate and question myself, *Did I let my kids take the place of where my wife should have been? Was I trying to recoup my childhood through them, knowing Bruce wasn't around to taint it this time?*

I remembered Dad's warning long ago about not marrying someone like Mom. I hadn't, but I learned the hard way that the quiet type can also sometimes be just as hurtful.

I never imagined in a million years that a divorce trial would be one of those trials I would ever have to face. Never could this sort of trial fit into the pure joy category for me. Since I was the man, I was the one who was ordered to move out. That meant without my children. Unfortunately, no matter how great of a dad I was, that's usually how it goes. Driving away with only my packed-up suitcase, and having to leave my three miracles behind, was the most excruciating loss I had ever felt. I couldn't even bear to look in the rearview mirror.

Broken down to nothing, I unlocked the door to a cold and empty apartment. It felt as if my pain was dominating every square foot of that tiny space.

That night, I crawled into my sleeping bag in the middle of the hard floor, and wept about how my daddy status had been taken from me. Never had I cried so deeply. The tears soaked my pillow. I had never felt so much loss. I physically hurt in my heart, and wanted to wail in sheer grief over them, but the walls were so thin, I didn't want anyone to hear me.

All I wanted was to sleep away my troubles. Barely dozing off, the angry voice of Bruce jolted my eyes wide open. I struggled to free myself from the hold of the sleeping bag. The zipper broke as I bolted up in a panic to run away from him. When I came to a dead stop by running into the wall, it woke me up. I dropped to my knees and began to weep again. My nightmares had returned.

Trying to calm myself, I crawled over to my sleeping bag and nestled back in, hoping to fall back to sleep. Having to turn my soaked pillow over, I lay my head down on the dry side to shut my eyes to what just happened.

Sleep hadn't returned when my alarm clock startled me. Rifling through my suitcase on the floor, I grabbed clothes to put on after my shower; but nothing could wash off the swollen red traces of distress on my face.

The long, drawn-out twelve days between my visitations with my children were wrenching. It was more like being stuck in solitary confinement. The little bit of dwindled-down daddy time I was given was like tossing scraps to a starving man. Visitation for me was spent refilling my time with them with new fragments of me they were missing at home.

My Friday night to pick them up finally came. When I knocked on the door to what used to be my house, I was excited to take them for a campout on the living room floor of my new apartment. Strangely,

I knew something was up when Brian, Benny, and Becca weren't in sight. It was obvious this was not going to be the typical exchange the parenting plan had designated.

Instead, I was handed a thick, stapled, paper stack of devastation—a Domestic Violence Order of Protection. The door shut on me, and I stood in silence on the doorstep. The little bit of life left in me had just been extinguished. A blunt, wide-open wound in my gut couldn't have been more painful. This meant CPS—Child Protective Services—was investigating. To my total surprise, the paperwork alleged I had molested my daughter. *This is not true! Where did this come from? Was it a far-fetched custody tactic? This is just wrong.* I would never in a million years impose on my children what happened to me. Going back to my apartment alone that night, all I could do was lay low and be quiet.

I was numb. But then, something happened that weekend. The scare of an accusation like that turned into a blessing for me. Reading what was in print on those papers tore the scab right off my own abuse.

Perhaps, this is what it probably took to break me out of my shell and rise up from underneath what happened to me.

As the investigation ran its course, I did a lot of praying. More praying than I had ever done before. My faith told me that God would reveal my innocence, so I wasn't worried. It was not seeing my children that was torture.

Another Friday night alone without my children. I was holding a carry-out box of leftovers from my party-of-one dinner out. Thirty days had passed since my life had been turned upside down, still waiting to hear something about the status of my case. Before I went in my apartment for the rest of my lonely weekend, I checked my mail. There was one letter waiting in the slot. I slid it out to read the return address: 'Child Protective Services.' *Well, this is it.* I put my box of food down and tore open the envelope. Shooting up a quick prayer, I started to slowly unfold it and skimmed down to the bottom to find the outcome of my fate. There it was . . . and . . . there I stood. In awe! Never had I imagined a nine-letter word could mean so much, 'UNFOUNDED!'

I sat down right there on the cement, and broke down in tears. I couldn't believe it. *Thank you, Lord.* Not only for the verdict, but how God was using this trial to shed some light on what was still in the dark for me. Needless to say, I got some much-needed sleep that night.

TWENTY-SIX

ASTRAY

JUST LIKE DIVORCE didn't agree with me, being single and alone didn't either. So, a record-time rebound relationship came searching for me. At least that's how I justified it anyway. There she was. Teaching in the same Sunday school class I was teaching in. Rachel was her name. One day, she flaunted her empty ring finger in front of my face. It took me long enough to wake up and realize she wanted me to know she was available. I was so mired up in my own chaos, her flirty gesture didn't register. I had been thrown to the curb so many times, I deliberately ignored any signs of what could have been a pickup line.

I don't know if she knew all what would come with marrying me, but just one month after my divorce was final, she didn't care, and married me anyway.

Rebound or not, Rachel saved my life. Blending a family of six children was not the issue; blending all the step-relationships and personalities was. No matter what challenges our blended family had, her children were a blessing. They filled a little bit of my place as a father when I couldn't be a full-time daddy to my own anymore. I tried to rejuvenate what they were missing too, but there was tremendous guilt on my part in doing so, as mine were now the ones who were missing out.

Within the first week, as always, having to adjust to my new surroundings disrupted my sleep routine. One early morning, a struggle with Bruce was transpiring in a nightmare; at the same time my alarm clock sounded. It felt so real, I swung a punch to get Bruce's choke-hold off me. My punch was actually my fist banging down on the clock to shut off the snooze button. Still deep in my nightmare, I flung myself out of bed. I tripped and hit my side full force on the corner of the nightstand, slicing it open. The pain jarred me awake and I felt the blood trickling down my leg. The throbbing that came on felt as if I had been attacked by some wild animal. That was Rachel's introduction to what it meant to be married to me.

The resulting two-inch scar marked an insignia defining Bruce's continued hold on me; one more obvious clue I still hadn't dealt with my past when he kept sneaking up on me in my present.

But, there was no time to concentrate on me. We had six kids to think about.

"The kids are going to be okay" cliché wasn't turning out to be true, especially for my boys. Their rebellion gave them permission to think they could do whatever they wanted. That took them in the wrong direction and they began hanging out with the wrong type of friends.

I tried my best to maintain my place as their dad, keeping Scouts front and center, remembering my promise to get them to Eagle Scout. But the limited time we spent together at Scouts, tied into their every other weekend visitation, was only a fraction of the time boys their age need from a father's influence.

Outside peer pressure became more alluring than our father-and son relationship. Their behavior wasn't matching the dreams I had for them. They started off smoking cigarettes, then graduated to marijuana. Not what I envisioned as a quality bonding time for brothers. Not what I envisioned for them at all.

Brian opted to couch surf at whichever friend's house had a vacancy.

Discipline was hopeless. He would sneak out, just to be returned home by the police after we reported his running away. Attempts to ground him was a joke. His smug disrespect was getting worse, and he'd turn right back around to repeat his tug-of-war behavior.

The brothers' influence on each other was way more enticing than mine. Their Scout Oath went by the wayside. And, then some. Benny became an apprentice to Brian's bad choices. They shadowed each other as if it were a competition. As the boys became increasingly sidetracked, any hopes I had of them following in my footsteps were crumbling.

My daily journal became an outlet for expressing my sadness and confusion. I penned desperate pleas of help for my sons. Doing what I had learned to do so well, I blocked out what was tearing up my life, got in my car, and headed off to work. I didn't know how to cope any other way.

As their shenanigans escalated, one night I got a phone call from the police telling me that one of my sons had been caught shoplifting at the local Safeway store. I sure couldn't block that one out of my head.

I just wanted to scream. As they both continued to go astray, I was scared to death of the black hole they were approaching that would eventually lead them to a labyrinth of no return. I begged God to intervene, but the boys' choices were taking over.

I'd be out all hours of the night searching for my prodigals. Exhaustion from sleep deprivation became part of my life. Twenty-four hours a day, my phone was on high alert as if were a taxi service. I should have just slept in my clothes. Calls in the night were constant reminders of the damage and destruction of divorce.

An invasion of evil was already overwhelming them. Their willpower was stolen. The pot issue was minor compared to what was coming. Addiction was gaining.

Devastated to see how far my boys had drifted, I had to learn the language of addiction. It was forced upon my family to learn—as it had become the norm around the house—and we fought like heck to not make it the norm for any of the other kids in the home. I had to stay strong.

The drugs became good at manipulating them; in turn, they became good at manipulating me. I knew tough love was tough, but it was necessary, even though it was harder on me.

No matter how many treatment programs they shuffled through, the routine became more of a habitual roller coaster, where the bind of their addiction grew tighter with each go around.

There was no time to dwell on it though. Trying to survive the heartache of what had become of them consumed all I had left, leaving only bits and pieces for the rest of the family.

TWENTY-SEVEN

DOUBLE WHAMMY

IT WAS A normal work day when I felt the vibration of my cellphone in my front pocket. I stopped what I was doing, and removed my earplugs. With all the calls about my boys, the phone had not been a friend of mine.

At almost the last buzz, I pulled it out to read the lit-up screen to see who was calling. *My brother?* I was surprised, as we rarely talked. If he was calling, it had to be important.

"Hey, Matt, how are you?" I said in my usual, laid-back manner. I jumped in my seat when he yelled out, "That sick faggot!" *He had to be ranting about Bruce.* His voice was intense. I wondered why he was way more amped up than usual.

Barely taking a breath, Matt fired away, "We are going after that pedophile." As a dark swarm of the past with Bruce flash-flooded inside me, I said, "Hold on, Matt. Give me a second." I walked over to an empty conference room, shut the door behind me, and sat down trying to steady myself.

I didn't know why he was so angry about Bruce?

Only in passing had Matt and I ever talked about what happened that night at the drive-in, when it was just him and me and Bruce. We downplayed it by making a "Scout's Honor" promise to never tell a soul.

Occasionally, when we were younger, we'd joke about what Bruce did. Our sarcasm was used as a cover to make sure we stayed '*morally straight,*' just as the Scout Oath required of us. For some reason, it never dawned on me that Bruce would ever try to mess around with Matt again.

I must have been wrong. The level of Matt's intensity made it sound as if it was more than just that one night.

"Out of curiosity, Matt," I bluntly asked, "How long did Bruce do this to you?"

"Uh, Tom, really?"

The cold sneer in his voice rattled me, as he went on.

"Don't tell me you didn't know we were both competing in the same double-whammy? Your turn, my turn, your turn, my turn. Bruce thought it was such a clever game working the two of us. Tom, you do realize he called me his Prize Scout too, right? He warned me not to tell you because it would upset you."

Matt's words puzzled me. *I thought I was Bruce's only Prize Scout.* We had always been beyond competitive with each other in everything, my brother and me. As the realization sank in of what Matt was telling me, I thought, *You're pitiful, Tom.*

Matt kept on unraveling the past, "Tom, do you remember that old Polaroid camera Bruce had?"

"No, I don't recall."

"What are you talking about, Tom? Are you serious? Don't you remember seeing the snapshot slide out, and the noise it made?"

Matt was so wound up, he could hardly get his next words out. "Bruce showed me the nudie pictures he snapped of you and compared them to mine."

I cringed as if my body had just taken a heavy hit. *How can I deny that? Matt is remembering stuff that I'm not.*

"Hey, I have to put you on hold for a minute," Matt said.

Stunned, I stood there with the phone in my hand. Matt's words made it obvious that my blocked brain had spared me from remembering all the details of the abuse. Matt hadn't been that lucky.

As I waited for Matt to come back on the phone, the stupid thought of how I had lost out on my Prize Scout ranking with Bruce kept sneaking back to harass me. I shook my head as if it would erase the thought.

Matt came back on the line and brought up a police report he had filed on Bruce a few years back. *Police report? What police report? I didn't know anything about it. Why hadn't he told me?*

"I wanted to see Bruce held accountable for what he had done," Matt stressed.

The threats Bruce made about killing my family had stuck with me. He knew what he was doing. It worked. Not a word told from either of us. Matt has always been the forward one. I am glad he had the gumption to do what I couldn't.

"Yeah, I was sure justice would be served if I got the police involved. Tom, I filed the report on behalf of both of us."

Then Matt brought up something that rattled me to my core. He asked, "Do you realize how many more victims of Bruce there must be and probably still are right now? How many more boys he has rocked his jollies off with?"

Matt got his hopes up when the detective who investigated the report determined that there was sufficient evidence for prosecution.

"Tom, with all of that in writing, it was validation right there that someone had listened to me. Confirmation that his twisted sex streak would be over when he was put away. All those years that creep thought he could get away with it. I would love to tell him face-to-face how I really feel, 'Just wait, Mr. Child Lover. A straight-jacket and padded room would be suitable for a maniac like you.'"

I could feel darkness gathering around Matt's words as he added, "He ought to be castrated as punishment for what he did." My mind was clouded with disgusting visual memories of Bruce, and his abuse. And now, I can see it meshed in with what Bruce probably did to Matt.

Matt began describing what the detective wrote down on the report about his visit to Bruce's home. Bruce was willing to openly discuss his history with the Scouts. Amazingly enough, he admitted having sex with the both of us.

Then, Bruce proceeded to nullify his actions by saying that he had since "found God."

Matt's voice got louder and angrier as he said, "It sure would have been great if he 'found God' before he went on his raping rampage with you and me, plus all the other countless boys he probably violated!"

Matt started talking about retaliation. I listened but was hesitant. Retaliation is not in my nature.

"Matt, why didn't the detective take Bruce's confession about abusing us more seriously? I'm a little baffled if his excuse of 'finding God' let him get away with it."

Matt quickly answered, "I wouldn't put it past Bruce to use the same mind control he used on us to play the detective."

Sociopath, narcissist, psycho? Whatever Bruce was, I knew Satan was involved and working overtime to lure even the police into his web. *Why not?* His deceptive ploys had worked quite well for him. Bruce was the smoothest of talkers, and what he said always slid by as believable.

The dark vibe in Matt's voice sharpened, "I was really looking forward to seeing his hands cuffed, and him booked into the county jail. It would only be a matter of time before he'd get what's coming to him . . . compliments of his fellow inmates. That's what they do in prison with pedophiles, you know?"

Matt said the detective's entry in the follow-up report ended with this observation, "Not once during the conversation did Bruce state or indicate that he had lost his attraction to younger boys, and appeared that his pedophilia had not waned."

Even with Bruce's confession, and Matt's report, the police still closed the case after a year-long investigation.

"You can see why I'm so angry!" Matt said.

That must have been the reason Matt had never mentioned anything about the police report before. *I could see that. What a letdown.*

The power of shame and humiliation associated with that man had a way of sneaking back in. But then, with the added failure of the law not taking any action to prosecute, gave Bruce free rein back to keep on doing it—leaving what he did to us acceptable.

I knew Matt was beating himself up. By the time he finally went to the police to file the report, the three-year statute of limitations had lapsed, resulting in no arrest. There were no charges. No prosecution. No jail time. No consequences. No nothing for what Bruce did! A measly three-year deadline had shut the case down. It no longer had any legal significance, and was concluded with a status of 'Cleared Exceptional.' The only thing the police could do was retain the information.

Like that was supposed to make us feel better.

And that is exactly why some don't come forward to report sexual abuse. When a victim bares all, just to be turned away because of some stupid time restraints, it leaves them feeling like they are treading on a tidal wave. I believe when a victim is stuck serving a life sentence of pain, why shouldn't the perpetrator?

Victims may not even remember the abuse until maybe decades later. Unfairly, the law only gives them a three-year window to recognize their abuse matters.

Bruce robbed the innermost part of me and my brother. How can a child molester, an admitted pedophile, be rewarded by walking free, while we paid the dues of the violation—our stolen childhoods?

The longer Matt and I talked, I thought, *Maybe I have more than just amnesia.* The possibility of *PTSD* came to mind. Listening to what Matt had uncovered, combined with the limited memories I did recall, post-traumatic stress disorder better matched the symptoms I struggled with.

At this point in the conversation, Matt sounded as if he could barely contain his fury. "There is no way I am going to condone that lame outcome."

I could hear in the background the smack of his fist pounding down. "Nobody is going to get away with threatening to kill my family while killing our childhoods in the process. A statute of limitations doesn't register with a Stewart. We were taught not to give into limitations. I intend to keep Bruce from doing this to anyone else."

Trying to defuse the tension, I joked, "You really remind me of Mother, Matt." Among the few good things that came out of her narcissistic teachings was how she taught us not to trip over ourselves while running full blast to the finish line. Funny thing though . . . she never mentioned watching out for anyone in the way you might plow over to get there.

The level of fear Bruce planted hadn't diminished in either of us. It had been a risky gamble to file a police report against Bruce in the first place; the odds were against us. I'd imagine the accusation hadn't sat well with Bruce.

My brother's call had brought the *"aim, fire, and shoot"* fear back to life for me, and was reason enough to finally tell my wife where all these nightmares came from.

TWENTY-EIGHT

FINALLY HEARD

TRYING TO ESCAPE the chaos of my life on the main floor of my house, I hid myself away upstairs with the door locked. There were only short durations of time I could sit long enough to think. Sitting at my desk, my brother's conversation about Bruce crossed my mind. I hadn't had any time to let his recall of it all sink in and, of course, that only lasted for about five minutes. I hoped the house would stay quiet long enough from the girls' screeching downstairs for me to answer the phone call that's ringing. It just happened to be Matt calling me again.

His angst was worrying me. I answered to his same anger in his tone again. *I don't ever remember him being this strung out about anything.* It was clear that his robust memory had much more forgetting to do than my absent-minded one.

In a hyped-up tone, he asked me, "Have you heard what's going on with the Catholic Church?"

"Uh, only in passing," I told him. "I overheard something about it." I was reluctant to admit how disconnected from society I was, so I gave him a noncommittal answer. I was too preoccupied sprinting through my own life. The upheaval and clamor never ceased with my boys, leaving me no time for interruptions from the outside world to add to the already huge mess inside.

Matt couldn't wait to tell me how it all came about, "I dropped my change into the newspaper vending machine, and snatched a Sunday paper off the top of the almost sold-out stack. I found a bench and sat down. My eyes immediately went to the headline at the top of the front page, 'Church Allowed Abuse by Priest for Years.' When I continued reading down the page, Tom, it felt like my own past was on that front page in print. Line by line, the story written about the pedophiles in the church and what they did to their victims was speaking right to me. I wanted to yell, 'Wait a minute, that's just what Bruce did.'"

Since I wasn't saying anything on my end, he paused now and then to make sure I was listening. "You with me, Tom?"

I was getting a little sidetracked thinking about how Bruce's abuse had chipped away at Matt's heart just as it had mine. *How could it not?* But Matt hadn't suppressed his feelings as I had. His scars were still raw and wide open to the elements. Mine were still buried underground for the most part. Neither one of us had found a happy medium.

Then I heard something different in Matt's words. I sensed his anger was subsiding.

His voice turned solemn. "Since the police report I filed came up empty, I started to believe that maybe Bruce's abuse was all just a figment of my imagination . . . Maybe I didn't matter." *Oh, wow, that's what I thought too.* "Maybe I was crazy, but seeing the story today about the priests and the Catholic Church shocked me, just like one of those heart defibrillators. It woke me up, Tom."

Matt reread the article over and over again, and felt the pain those poor boys suffered. Then it hit him like a brick. "Tom, I shouted out loud—that's me! That's what happened to us! I was angry for them. I was angry for us."

He hadn't cared who was around, or who heard him holler like some kook.

"You know, Tom, someone heard their cries. Someone listened to them! Someone believed them!"

The parallels went without saying. The secret Boy Scout abuse was a literal rehashing of the secret church abuse. Authority figures used their position to groom their victims, brainwash, and abduct the innocence of their victims.

In our case, two brothers were sitting ducks—raised as ideal targets for a pedophile.

This sickening epidemic has to be stopped. How could any priest of God desecrate the Lord's name by such blasphemy? Then again, how could Scoutmasters do the same as they had sworn as a Scout to do their duty under God? The only difference between the Boy Scouts and the church is Scouts wear uniforms—altar boys wear robes.

I broke in with, "Matt, what about the statute of limitations? Bruce got away with what he did even after he was turned in."

Gathering up his confidence, Matt said, "I've already reached out to a victims' rights attorney who specializes in child abuse like what's happened with the Catholic Church. Bruce himself may be exempt, but fortunately, the Boy Scouts of America are not!"

"Get this, Tom, the law firm's motto is, 'Yesterday's Children Saving Today's Children.'"

When Matt said those words, I felt their impact. I knew right away God was giving the go-ahead. It was as if those words came to me from God himself.

"Matt, you're right. We are those kids from yesterday. We have to be the voice for the ones who can't or won't speak for themselves. We have to protect the ones who might be next in line."

When we hung up, we were both pumped that we could do this together. Through Matt's phone call, God was not only giving me confirmation, He was revealing the good that could come out of our abuse—our lost childhood at the hands of a pedophile.

My abuse had a purpose. I had a story to tell. I wanted to turn Bruce's evil into good, and to save many lives by sharing what God was going to do with the suffering of two brothers.

The day Matt and I walked into the lawyer's office for our consultation, I wasn't sure what to expect. My first impression of Tim Kosnoff was positive. I was in awe of this distinguished looking man who could be the key to unlocking our past. We were grateful he was even taking the time to listen. Not being believed by my own mother was disappointment enough, making me that much more hesitant to take the chance again. Proud to be sitting there next to my brother, I admired Matt's passion and spirit for getting us that far. Without him, I knew I would not have come forward. In detail, Matt started reciting from his photographic memory the extent of who Bruce was and what he did. My memory stirred up the same vulgar acts, the same obscure places, and the same vicious threats. It could have been my recollection talking the same as my brother's. What Bruce did to Matt, he did to me. I sat there thinking, If I remembered in detail all that Matt remembers, I might not have survived long enough to be sitting here today.

"Taking on the Boy Scouts is going to be difficult," Tim warned us. "It's like chopping down a sequoia tree with a pocketknife."

"Nothing is too much of a challenge for a Stewart," Matt said. We looked at each other and broke out in laughter. We had to share with Tim how we had to give credit to our mother for instilling that in us, no matter how many waves she left in her wake.

When we left Tim's office, it felt as if healing in us had begun. Once and for all, we could also say, "We have finally been heard." Like the abused altar boys, someone had heard our cries; someone had listened to us; someone had believed us.

TWENTY-NINE

RED FLAGS

TWELVE MONTHS OF fact-finding lay ahead. We had much research to do to build a case. Homework of sorts. We began familiarizing ourselves with what was already known about abuse in the Boy Scouts. Our attorney recommended the book entitled *'Scout's Honor'* by Patrick Boyle. The author quoted this hard truth, "These files are an incredible treasure trove of information about how child molesters operate in youth-serving organizations."

In the book, I learned in-depth about the history and reality of widespread molestation in the Scouts. It was even worse than I expected. The book exposed how a deliberate 100-year cover-up was camouflaged by some so-called secret files. Worse yet, loose tabs were kept on these files. Any suggestion or proof of abuse would be hushed and hidden. These tactics did little to protect the boys who were overlooked while the Boy Scouts of America protected its name. Matt and I began to gather any background information on Bruce volunteering in the Boy Scouts that we could get our hands on. More importantly, any records that might reveal Bruce's misbehavior within the Scouts.

We did obtain some very damning evidence with Bruce's name on it, and then some with Bruce's name mysteriously off. The specific file we attempted to request from the troop that Bruce was still active in was mysteriously missing. Yes, Bruce was still active! Those were the first red flags that were waved in front of our faces.

My job was to reach out to the person who should have known about the odd goings on with Bruce more so than anyone else—the man to whom Bruce was assistant Scoutmaster under when I was in their troop as a Boy Scout.

I squeezed in time to pay him a visit, traveling across the state to where he had moved. Our meeting turned a little awkward after I filled him in on why I was there. He immediately told me, "Make sure you are only going after Bruce and not the Scouts." It was obvious to me he was protecting the Boy Scouts of America. I continued to ask him questions as tactfully as I could without revealing my full motives. But from then on, his answers seemed defensive. He hadn't noted anything out of the ordinary. He seemed to be protecting himself from any blame by association. I chalked up the interview as another cover-up.

Then Matt did something very daring, coming as it did twenty years after the fact. He personally went to see Bruce at his house. Bruce was holding vital information and we needed it to proceed. That alone gave him the courage to go.

Bruce's wife answered the door and gladly let him in. Matt sat across from the now unemployed Bruce and his wife by his side. He was determined to be as discreet as possible by starting out with general conversation and small talk. Bruce's wife had no clue as to why Matt was there.

He knew how much of a risk it was going there, but kept it generic to keep the peace. If Bruce had known the real reason for the visit, the gun case might have been opened to scare Matt out of his house.

After a while, the conversation went dim, telling Matt it was time to leave. Before he did, Matt invited Bruce outside alone so he could get down to the core of his visit. If there was anyone who was creative enough to play a little mind game with Bruce to get the information he needed, it was Matt.

"Bruce, I need some closure in my life about what happened between us. I need to hear from you how you see it."

Right away, Bruce launched into what seemed to be a carefully rehearsed account, "At the time with you and Tom, I had a demon living inside of me, and he was the devil."

Matt told me later he was annoyed by his strange reasoning. Bruce was falling back on his excuse of how he had changed after he had found God, just as he claimed in the police report.

Matt struggled to keep quiet. He didn't dare say out loud that he didn't believe a word Bruce was saying. He was waiting on Bruce's next concocted story as to when the supposed devil left his body.

The findings on the police report showed Bruce had confessed to relations with a nameless boy just five years prior to that. Since Bruce's sudden exorcism contradicted his confession, right away Matt was tempted to ask him how many more were out there.

Bruce continued to ramble on about having a sex addiction . . . and how he was looking for love in all the wrong places. *Well, no kidding!*

It all sounded to Matt like a shallow rendition of what resembled the echo of a counseling session.

Bruce said he had sought out psychiatric help. More than likely, it was prompted by the police report and not by his conscience. He said the psychiatrist felt his addiction was due to a lack of love in his life. Bruce shared his own conclusion—how his attraction for boys equated his longing for love. *Sick!*

Matt couldn't help but resent Bruce's rationalizations. He refrained from telling Bruce what he really felt to his face. *For at least the last thirty years or so; you crazed creep, you selfishly and relentlessly had no problem replenishing your so-called lack of love by stealing it from little boys like me who couldn't defend themselves.*

After listening to enough of Bruce's mumbo-jumbo, he realized he needed some genuine closure after all. He stood, towering over Bruce's shorter stature, and asked him straight up, "Are you sorry, Bruce?"

"Yes," Bruce said. Matt questioned his sincerity, but needed to hold on to something, even if it was only a little bit believable.

"Bruce broke off the conversation telling me, 'I need to get back to my wife. She's not comfortable with you being here.'"

All at once, it hit Matt. His anger flared as he realized Bruce's confession about being sorry meant nothing. *"Lying piece of garbage."* Matt had to use all his self-control not to unload on Bruce how uncomfortable he made the two of us feel by his abuse. Thankfully, he managed to keep his mouth shut. Matt reluctantly shook Bruce's hand and watched that poor excuse of a man walk back into his house.

As Matt drove away, that glimmer of closure he had hoped for faded. He said that he wished he could just let it all go. The visit did not help him at all, it made things worse. It created more resentment than what was already eating him alive.

By his own words that day, Bruce made it crystal clear how demented he still was.

From Bruce's house, Matt came directly over to my house to fill me in. "I had to see you, Tom, and tell you all the pathetic bunk that poured out of Bruce's mouth."

"Bruce whined about how us Stewart boys were, in his oddly old fashioned words, 'of studly athletic form.' While Bruce was comparing himself to us, he sulked about how short and pudgy of an outcast he was. When did envy ever become acceptable to justify sexual abuse?"

What he couldn't wait to tell me was how Bruce had the audacity to say, "It was your brother's idea to involve you sexually, Matt."

I couldn't believe it! "That's sure news to me." So; not just envy, but how did shifting blame become acceptable to justify sexual abuse?

Then I filled in the rest for Matt. "Let me guess. He must have reiterated his all-time favorite reasoning, 'What child wouldn't enjoy that type of pleasure?'"

Matt said, "It took all of my strength to stomach the rest of the lies he spewed through that scraggly, pedophile beard."

"I can't believe he is still free," I said. Bruce had weaseled right past everyone just like the snake he is.

Of course Bruce said he was "Sorry." Bruce was whacked enough to successfully brainwash himself.

This clarified our direction for our case. Together Matt and I gained strength as we prepared for what was ahead. The attorneys would use Bruce's confession to come against the Boy Scouts' negligence. Their disregard to known pedophile leaders who preyed on the boys who were supposed to be protected. No situation is more ideal for a child molester than this. Start them out young, reel them in through obedience and submission, and coerce them through the ranks by rewarding them with praise and badges.

While I was doing some research, I ran across some very damaging news archives. On May 18, 1935, *The New York Times* published an article about an existing problem titled: "Boy Scouts' 'Red Flag List' Bars Undesirables." The article disclosed a "red flag list" was being maintained by the Boy Scouts of America of "persons regarded as undesirable influences on youth." In the article, at the time, Colonel Theodore Roosevelt told the twenty-fifth anniversary meeting of the Scouts National Council, "We want to preserve fineness. We must choose between Scouts and hoodlums."

These facts are deplorable. What good did this "red flag list" from 1935 do anyway? It sure didn't protect us or any other boys.

Digging deeper, I found another article from 1991. A *Washington Times* investigation into the Boy Scouts revealed this: "The Boy Scouts are a magnet for men who want to have sexual relations with children . . . Pedophiles join the Scouts for a simple reason: it's where the boys are."

We were those same boys. This supposedly safe haven for boys turned out to be a place where the reputation and name of the Boy Scouts of America was more important than our safety.

From what I found, the Boy Scouts have been aware they were dealing with pedophiles for almost a century, but thought the obstacle course they constructed was sufficient.

I thought about the many other boys who have suffered and continue to suffer in silence. This is exactly why we were bringing the lawsuit. Victims had paid the price of their childhoods for the sake of the Boy Scouts of America saving its image. All the while, the self-image of victims had been ripped away and shredded. Some had turned to drugs, alcohol, pornography, or, worse yet, committed pedophilia themselves. Fueled by what came out of Bruce's sick mind, we needed to be heard. Especially for the ones who thought they were broken beyond repair, and chose suicide to solve their pain.

Bruce just makes me sick!

THIRTY

UNDER OATH

BEFORE WE COULD file the lawsuit, I had one thing left I needed to do. It was highly doubtful the Boy Scouts of America would appreciate me continuing as Scoutmaster if I was taking them to court. It was an agonizing decision, but unavoidable.

Reluctantly, I walked in to what would be my last troop meeting, wearing my Scout uniform that would soon be hung up for good.

My farewell announcement began with appreciation expressed for the coleaders, parents, and all my Scouts. Then it was time to drop the bomb.

I faced the troop and said, "As your Scoutmaster, I regret to inform you that I am resigning from my position in this troop."

The sighs in the room hurt me as I knew they would. For the first time in public, I spoke about my abuse that happened to me as a boy as tactfully as I could. I did not attach Bruce's name to my story, but I did caution the real risks of abuse in the Scouts. I told the boys never to keep a secret such as that. My closing words left no room for debate, as I announced, "I can no longer participate as a leader in an organization that does not protect boys." The room went silent as I walked out the door.

Superior Court Case #03-2-37274-9 would soon be considered the first of its kind, a landmark case against the Boy Scouts of America, the foundation to reveal what the American Public had a right to know. Matt called it a "David versus Goliath battle." We thought the prior year of preparation was grueling—it was nothing compared to what we were in for. It began as a media frenzy with the news coverage of our press conference announcing the filing of our lawsuit.

The Boy Scouts of America were tough and promised to get tougher. They are a huge institution padded with what seemed to be indestructible armor and unlimited resources to use in their defense. We had nearly a hundred years of abuse to prove, so our strategy needed to be a smoking-hot, loaded weapon to gain any leverage against them. We knew what it was—we just needed to get it. The Scouts would eventually drag us through some major hurdles that prolonged our goal of discovering what they were keeping under wraps. Their efforts to protect the century-long masquerade was a benefit only to the pedophiles themselves and the dignity the American public assumed the Boy Scouts of America had. Matt's and my combined twenty-two years of abuse seemed to mean little to an organization that wanted only to save face—not to save boys.

We were two brothers, born in the same family, with the same upbringing, experiencing the same circumstances, and the same abuse. *The truth will always come out,* I'd tell myself. Part of that truth coming out is usually the result of someone's courage. We Stewarts were ready to ride this hurricane out to help navigate the less apt or more afraid to calmer waters.

It was time for us to submit our personal declarations. We were to disclose the hardcore particulars and reveal what Bruce was capable of.

I had never written down any specifics about what Bruce did to me before then. With my blank sheet of graph paper lit up by the lamp at the corner of my desk, it didn't take long for the memories to drain down to the paper. The neatly aligned block letters satisfied my compulsive engineer habits that helped steer me on this assignment.

The words came easier than I expected, but my emotions had a much more difficult time catching up. Battling the chaos of my dysfunctional marriage, my addicted sons, and the complex family dynamics of the varied last names of my blended family had stripped the emotion out of me. The weight from my muddled life—now tangled up with the stress of the court case—was brutal. I was hard-pressed from all sides, including my work and the necessary overtime I was putting in to keep up with my depleted finances. No wonder I didn't give myself time to open up my feelings. I didn't have the time or the energy.

But I did hold on to my faith—the only thing that could sustain a life like mine. With all what God had brought me through thus far, my time with Him was never compromised. I'd find a secluded spot somewhere early each morning—usually before the sun came up, the only time I could be still long enough to pray for that grace in my life.

One morning, bright flashing lights pulled up behind my car and interrupted my devotional time. The officers looked amused when I said, "Hi, officer, I'm just praying and reading my Bible."

One officer jokingly said, "I'm glad you are one step ahead, sir, and prepared by prayer, because you are going to need it in this neighborhood." I finished up my reading with a huge smile on my face for the unique way God brings witnessing opportunities.

Next were the court-ordered psychological evaluations and counseling sessions. The attorneys for the Scouts were doing what they could to prove beyond a shadow of a doubt that Matt and I had turned out just fine.

Then came the three, eight-hour-long depositions for each of us. On one side of the eight-foot-long conference table sat my attorney and me. Sitting on the other side were the attorneys for the Boy Scouts. All females. Their strategy was to intimidate us out of baring all the down-and-dirty details in front of women.

But it was who came in next that they thought would be their best secret weapon. Seated directly across from me, he was in the perfect position to stare me down. The short, plump, bearded and balding, unkempt bully himself, *Bruce Phelps*.

Their tactic of menacing me into submission wasn't going to work. I wasn't going to let it.

My posture straightened up. I took a sip of water from the full glass in front of me and cleared my throat, ready to answer whatever they had to throw at me. Swearing to tell the truth, the whole truth, and nothing but the truth, my "So help me God" meant everything to me.

As time ticked slowly by, my answers to their questions about the man I was looking at drew me back to when he was my Scout leader. He didn't wear a beard back then, but I saw the same eyes behind those thick glasses. The longer I sat there, the more lucid the past I had with Bruce became.

The tedious hours were necessary to prove his guilt, but the further we got along in the day, something else was also happening in the process. The same strange fading of animosity I had experienced at his wedding was happening again.

When the deposition portion was almost over, I was relieved. It was getting more difficult to fire darts at him. What a troubled individual he was; I felt sorry for him.

I knew with all the trauma I had gone through, there would have been no way I could have come out the other side intact if I had allowed anger and resentment to take over my life.

Our reason for bringing this suit was to fight against the neglect of the Scouts, not to bury Bruce. Maybe he had truly found God like he said he had. If he truly had, I prayed he wouldn't get lost again.

As we were wrapping up, I suddenly felt an overwhelming desire to forgive this man. We made eye contact before he left the room, and it sure felt like I had. But, it couldn't have come from my will. I never thought a man like that was forgivable. I was wrong. God can do anything . . . and I know that He did it to free me.

Bruce's deposition was next on the calendar. He walked in sporting a classy suit and tie like a real gentleman would. More like "*genital*" man.

We needed honesty from him. Would he tell the truth because he was under oath? He swore to do so. Much to our surprise, he did. Well, most of the truth anyway—enough to baffle skeptics on both sides of the table.

Later, I was given the opportunity to watch Bruce's deposition on video tape. It was good I did not attend his actual deposition; otherwise, I may not have been able to maintain my composure when I heard some of the answers he gave. I know for sure Matt couldn't have. His outlandish excuses were, "It was Matt's idea to be with me." "Tom just didn't understand and asked me to show him." No matter how far-fetched Bruce's answers were, they were enough to seal his guilt, even if he believed his answers were justified.

THIRTY-ONE

UNDER WRAPS

BRUCE HAD BEGUN his sex streak sometime in the sixties. Sexual abuse had been running rampant since the beginning, but no one outside of the perpetrators, the victims, maybe some parents, and a fleet inside of the organization keeping it quiet and tucked away, was aware of it.

Straight from the mouth of Bruce; relayed through his attorney, Bruce unveiled how he ticked, and how he got away with it by explaining how easy it had been for a pedophile to "graze in the wide-open pastures of the Boy Scouts as they search for lost sheep to devour."

He was asked what he knew about Scout leader rules in relation to Scouts.

He started out, "I am really not aware of any rules that were in place that I avoided or evaded. It was a different time back then, and the organization did not seem—at least outwardly—to be thinking about how to ensure that children were not abused. They just needed the help."

Bruce continued with, "One of the main reasons Scoutmasters were able to abuse Scouts was the lack of parental involvement. Many parents thought of scouting as a type of child care that took some of the burden of parenting off them. Jokingly, the BSA were also were referred to as the 'Baby Sitters of America.'"

In another question, Bruce was asked, "What type of conduct by a leader should have raised concerns, even in the absence of any complaints being lodged?"

Bruce answered, "Mainly the amount of time a Scoutmaster spent alone with kids, away from sanctioned scouting activities. Another red flag should have been the degree to which individual attention was paid to a particular boy."

It was most interesting how Bruce dumped his blame over onto the Scouts, and even the parents, in the same way that he shifted the blame to Matt and me. But, that's exactly what we needed. We couldn't go after Bruce, but his confession as to how he used the faults of the Scouts to his advantage proved our point.

The hard truth is that the Boy Scouts have been susceptible to sexual predators like Bruce since the organization was established over a hundred years ago. Being the perfect stomping ground for pedophiles, habitual oversights gave way for pedophiles to simply swoop up their defenseless targets and fulfill their urges with no questions asked.

That's how it worked for Bruce.

We were elated when our subpoena to obtain the files was approved by the judge. In turn, the Scouts appealed. We climbed a step higher, the Scouts appealed again. We stomped on their toes yet another step higher, and they appealed again. Tim was right. A case against the Boy Scouts was like "chopping down a sequoia tree with a pocketknife." But, their unrelenting legal efforts were shining a bright light on their guilt. *What were they hiding?*

Their final chance to appeal brought us straight to the top—The Washington State Supreme Court. No appeal would be allowed at this level, and all became in our favor. The Scouts were ordered to hand these files over for only our attorneys to see. This was huge. We had our hot smoking gun.

The information our attorney discovered within these files was unfathomable. The released files revealed the scanned documents noting actual or suspected abuse occurrences. The devastating aspect was how the victimized boys were hushed in order to protect the presumably good name of Scouts. The documents themselves were bare-bones proof that lurid information had been kept private, internally. That damning information would have been hibernating indefinitely if we hadn't come along. Cases of abuse in the Scouts were not reported, investigated, or turned over to the police. Instead, the accused were quietly dismissed at the astronomical rate of one every three days.

More attention and care was directed at keeping it all under wraps, handled with the greatest of confidence and care, while what had happened to the victims was not. The impact on the survivors was downplayed, where counseling was offered as sufficient means to help them.

The most unsettling part was that from all the pedophiles listed in that twenty-year stretch, Bruce's name was nowhere to be found. It is terrifying to think how he slid under so many noses for all those years as a Scout leader. *How many other Bruces are out there who got away with what they imposed?*

In some cases, the accused were allowed to continue with just a warning. In other instances, when they were dismissed, the displaced men outsmarted the Scouts by packing up and moving elsewhere by quickly reapplying to a different troop under a different name, or just switch out a middle initial. That's all it took for the abuse to continue.

It was mass deception, and was unclear if their so-called "Red Flag" list was even referenced to extract any of the crooked ones. The files included a document from 1972 in which a BSA executive stated, "Legal action could only injure the Boy Scouts of America. My personal opinion is, 'If it don't stink, don't stir it.'"

Particularly, the Scouts failed by not performing background checks. I know this firsthand, as they didn't do one on me when I took on the role of Scoutmaster in my sons' troop. Even if background checks were conducted, leaders were still given the go-ahead to start immediately before the results came back. Unfortunately, the drawback of an organization dependent on volunteers was the lack itself. Also; considering the commitment of time required for those positions, it appeared the regard for background checks was not as important as filling the need.

THIRTY-TWO

PERVERSION FILES

THE BOY SCOUTS knew their fate was inevitably closing in on them. With the files in our hands, obviously, they didn't want them to go public . . . so, they proposed a settlement with us to make it all go away.

After three years and five months going back and forth; exhausted, we were urged to make a decision: either continue to move forward and risk the outcome, or settle. Washington State does not award punitive damages, and it may have been tricky convincing a jury in our favor over the Boy Scouts of America—no matter how much proof we had. We were also advised that since Matt was 6'7" and I was 6'3", it would also have been most difficult to convince any jury that we were defenseless and helpless. Presumably, as two professionals, our overall demeanor would tend to create an argument that Bruce's abuse was not mentally devastating to either of us.

Rather than going into a long court battle with an unpredictable outcome, we agreed to settle out of court in 2007, ending with no trial.

I was relieved, as my energy was gutted. What was left of my dysfunctional family structure was fragile, and would have been detrimental to drag them through the media circus of a trial.

It was never about any financial compensation; no amount could have ever bought back my innocence. I was there for what we actually did walk away with—the freedom to tell my story without a gag order. Since we didn't go to trial, the files obtained by our attorney were required to be returned to the Boy Scouts, stalling them from public release.

Miraculously, our landmark case set in motion what needed to continue. A lawsuit filed in the state of Oregon, following our out-of-court settlement, did go to trial and prevailed. Rooted in our initial discovery, both cases precipitated some of the Boy Scouts' greatest fears: exposing clear evidence and proof showing the sexual abuse epidemic in the Scouts. They could no longer hide behind their name. Made public in 2012, The Oregon Supreme Court mandated the Boy Scouts of America to release 20 years' worth—equaling 20,000 pages—of documented confidential files, revealing over 1,200 names of suspected and confirmed pedophiles and the abuse they committed for the years of 1965 through 1985, also referred to as the "Perversion Files." Some more recent files after 1985 have been revealed through a handful of court cases. The files from 1991 to present, and files prior to 1965, are still hidden, or have been destroyed.

The compilation of those files represents the largest and most comprehensive data collection on child sexual abuse by any one organization. What the Boy Scouts did to maintain the files may be comprehensive, but what the Boy Scouts failed to do is incomprehensible.

In their less than effective attempt to tackle the magnitude of the problem, the Scouts implemented a much-delayed effort to help in taking up some of the slack in protecting youth.

Youth Protection training was put in place in the late eighties to educate staff and volunteers, and mandate strict leadership screening through background checks, extensive training, and mandatory reporting of child abuse. Two-deep leadership has also been adopted, meaning, no one-on-one association between adults and youth.

However, as it stands now, because the Scouts have yet to release files from 1991 through to the present, it is unknown whether or not the training has improved the situation at all.

In my eyes, God's purpose for "The saving of many lives" is coming to fruition. Matt's and my purpose was to help protect those who had yet to fall victim to abuse by detouring any pedophiles who might try to enter the Scouts. Also, to bring awareness about any unknown pedophiles who might still be lurking about, just like a wandering Bruce-type of molester. As well as encourage any other muted "Tom and Matts" out there to come forward.

Thank you, Lord, for giving me my answer.

THIRTY-THREE

LOST FOOTING

AMAZED AT WHAT God had done in my life; I was especially amazed with the miracle of Him using my pain to expose the Scouts. I was pleased to get back to normal, starting with my family. Yet, with so much extended distraction, I conveniently forgot that normal was not my reality.

I found my refuge at church away from the rigmarole. Every Sunday morning, I'd find my way to my usual seat, front row, over to the right. Unfortunately, the seats saved next to me for my family became empty. Endless prayers seemed to get caught up in the reality of my dissolving marriage.

Trying to pretend nothing was wrong, as I always did, the issues with my boys became front and center, and my marriage went by the wayside.

I thought the bad experiences should have ceased with me, so they wouldn't be passed down to them. I prayed constantly for relief. *Lord, I would have taken on any sacrifice to protect them.*

But the next generation of Stewart brothers were wallowing through their own living hell. Different from the hell that Matt and I lived, but it was hell just the same.

Brian lost all interest in high school. There was no desire left in him to even continue to achieve his diploma. Drugs had robbed him of all motivation, and dulled his genius-level IQ. He settled for a GED.

His lifestyle and association with the wrong crowd landed him back in detox again for thirty days. From there, I gave him no choice but to sit in the passenger seat as I drove him straight down to the Salvation Army Adult Rehabilitation Center in Oregon for a six-month rehab program. He finished it and graduated in recovery. No matter how much ice and snow covered the freeway that winter, nothing was going to stop me from traveling the three hours to attend and congratulate him.

But his clean slate was temporary. He was again homeless and joy-riding life on the streets. When he contracted MRSA in his arm, I was hit with the naked truth that he was shooting up heroin. It didn't take his life, but his entire forearm was riddled by disfiguring scars, proof how close he came to death.

I had dreamed we'd be a father-and-son team that one day would stand up in front of hundreds of people talking about how he got free from drugs, and how they could too. His arm would be valuable visual proof for those who might be teetering towards the druggie side of life. The outward damage was bad, but only a fraction of what was going on inside.

Like his brother, high school also lost all appeal for Benny. He too settled for a GED. And, like his brother again, Benny's destination was the Salvation Army Rehabilitation Center, followed by the chance to change his life in Job Corps. It was my glimmer of hope and a great opportunity for him to achieve. And that's what he did—by obtaining his high school diploma.

Unfortunately, both of them had lost their footing again. My stomach would clench when my thoughts drifted to how much further my boys had lost their way. My dreams of them attending college crashed. Their futures had slipped right out from underneath them. I didn't understand. My brother and I had both graduated as valedictorians. I guess their little footprints that were supposed to follow in mine stumbled right off the page.

Brian had moved back from Oregon and got a job and an apartment. Things were looking up. I met him for dinner that weekend hoping to see signs he was still sober. I could see how drained he was, but didn't want to outright ask him if he was still clean.

No more than fifteen minutes had gone by in our meal when my phone rang. It was my wife. I excused myself from the table and took the call outside. I had the same feeling of dread in my gut as when my first wife dumped me. I was right.

After a six-week, in-house separation, she moved out and moved on with her life.

Lord, haven't I had enough? I've really had enough.

Lonely and by myself, feeling like a dumped loser again, I asked myself, *Why does this keep on happening to me? First divorce . . . I lose my kids. Second divorce . . . I lose my stepkids?*

It's been a lifetime full of what feels like betrayal in every facet of my life, beginning with my mother, her verbal abuse, Bruce and his sexual abuse, cancer, divorce, allegations, drug addicted children, and divorce again?

THIRTY-FOUR

TOUGH LOVE

IT WAS ANOTHER one of my lonely Friday nights, I was trying to keep myself occupied and keep my mind busy, so I headed for the church. I assumed that I was going to be the only one there so I could wallow in my pity in the sanctuary, but God had other plans. By His chance, Rene' just happened to be there wallowing in her own pity. I had known her for a few years prior through the friendship of our daughters. By God's chance, it was my soon to be ex-wife who invited Rene' to attend the church in the first place . . . we were both glad she did. That night, I was so very thankful that was the case. We laughed about how it all came about.

In the hour and a half that we talked, Rene' changed my life. She consoled the innermost part of me that was hurting so badly—leaving no doubt how equally-yoked we were. I fell in love with her that night. God sure knew what He was doing . . . as He always does with me. Prior to His divine appointment, my intentions were to hold off on dating altogether. Well . . . that didn't happen.

She was in no way another one of my in-record-time rebound relationships. She was a blessing God had delivered to me.

I didn't hesitate on asking her to accompany me on what would be our first date. I couldn't have dreamed of a better connection. It was magical.

But since I wasn't fully divorced yet, I knew I needed to ask for our pastor's permission if I could continue to date her. I didn't know what to expect since my divorce wasn't final—but I knew that this incredible man of wisdom had the perfect answer. With his blessing of, "God has already released you, Tom," convinced me that it just took me awhile longer to find the right one for me. His approval led to our second and third dates which turned into my proposal of marriage.

Rene' said, "Yes!"

Until my divorce was final and we could be married, I had to face coming home to my big empty house.

The silence seemed to bounce off itself. But it gave me plenty of space to think about how I could possibly help my sons.

It occurred to me they could move in until my wife to-be could. My hope was to give them another chance to get their lives together with me right there. In my denial, I hoped their addiction would not move back in with them. But my hope alone was not strong enough. It didn't take long to realize my mistake. I wasn't prepared for the appendages of the drug world that appeared under my roof. Items of value would soon start coming up missing. My house became a hazardous waste area. I never knew what I might find hiding underneath their mess. Fitted with industrial rubber gloves, I inspected their rooms, sifting through the mess they created for any drug paraphernalia that might have been smuggled in.

I didn't want to face what I found—blackened spoons and tinfoil, pen caps, empty prescription bottles, and plastic baggies with white residue. That was hard enough. But when a bright, orange-capped syringe I heard bouncing around in the dryer fell out to the ground, it became real.

When three more used syringes with exposed needles almost pricked my fingers, it left me no choice. The boys couldn't stay. I gave them a choice—rehab again or the streets.

Brian chose the streets. Benny thankfully chose rehab, and then would head to an Oxford House after.

Doing what I had to do, the locks had to be changed on the house. I never knew what was coming next or what to expect, and I had to put my foot down, restricting them from coming near the property completely.

I groaned the day I found Benny sleeping in his car in the driveway. Up in arms and confused . . . *but, he was doing so well when I went to see him?* For the first time, he admitted to my face he had been kicked out of the clean and sober house for not staying clean and sober.

It was incredibly hard when I had to tell him, "I'm sorry, Son, you can't stay."

One Saturday, a few weeks later, I was up on the hill by the road, doing yard work next to the barn on the property. The howl of the weed eater was muffled by my earplugs. Being outside helped me escape to a place where all was perfect . . . Mother always taught me how to fake it so well; at times, I could pretend that my life went there too.

The weed eater was sputtering, telling me it was running out of gas, so I shut off the motor to refill it.

I noticed a car pull off on the side of the road behind me, slowly braking toward where I was standing. I was so surprised to see Benny sitting in the passenger seat. He was in the car of a friend's whom I hadn't met before. His big, bright smile opened up to me as he stepped out of his side of the car. Removing my earplugs, I couldn't wait to hug him. I was so excited to see him, but it also made me sad.

He crunched through the gravel and came over to hug me with one of his big, warming hugs that could sweep anyone off their feet.

He looked happy. He said, "I was hoping you would be home, Dad. I wanted to stop by really quick and tell you something."

His words were as sincere as I had ever heard him. He looked at me and told me, "Dad, I don't know what I ever would have done without you. I would be dead without you. Thank you for putting your foot down. I'm going back into treatment."

I was speechless as his words melted me. With both of us crying, I told him, "I love you, and I'm so proud of you." I squeezed him so tight, like a child hugging a favorite teddy bear . . . *My Buddy.*

Standing there, savoring my moment with him, I could pretend for at least a little while that drugs never came and kidnapped my son.

As I watched him leave, I blinked away my tears. I wanted to run after him, but I dropped to the ground and sobbed as if it was the last time I was ever going to see him. Sitting on the pebbled dirt, I leaned up against the metal gate, thinking how the worry of a father never ends.

But I hadn't heard from Brian at all. The hardest thing for me to do was to not cave in when he did call. That's what I did best . . . cave in. I had to get over being concerned if he was going to get mad at me for sticking to my guns. It was a constant battle being a parent. A broken parent at that.

I had to admit that my approval addiction was just as much of a problem as their drug addiction. The patterns were identical. It was either the need to feel loved, or the need for drugs—seek, find, receive, regret, withdrawal . . . and repeat. *I need a daddy-do-over.* Wishing I could start my role as a father all over again.

I was grateful though to at least have been given another chance to start my role as husband over again. In front of her family and many great friends, we were married by our two favorite pastors. Rene's children stood up for us. Her two boys on my side, her two girls on her side. From day one, they had been loving and respectful. I was fortunate to not go through any stepparent rejection as my wife had to.

That day was the happiest day of my life; besides the birth of my children. Still, as I looked around at Rene's children standing by us, and my children were not there, a sadness crept in and their absence hurt like hell. I so wished they could have been there to see how happy I was to finally marry a woman who truly loved me as I loved her.

But I brushed aside my sadness and smiled as Rene' and I promised the last marriage vows either of us would ever speak again.

THIRTY-FIVE

MY BUDDY

I HAD BEEN up most of the night thinking about the sermon preached the day before. With my new wife sitting next to me filling the empty seat, the pastor was relaying the chaplain side of his job—the most difficult parts. He said the hardest part was having to tell parents their child was not coming home. When he talked about how many doors he had knocked on to tell parents their kids had overdosed and didn't make it, I could feel the pain through in my bones. I cringed as my own sons were living on the wild side of that same edge.

I couldn't fathom what those parents must go through, and what it must be like for him to deliver that kind of devastation. I watched as his face dropped when he said, "You don't ever want it to be me knocking on your door in my chaplain's uniform."

I shut my eyes as my heart was throbbing, thinking about my boys. I was thankful that a knock like that had not come to my door.

All the way to work that Monday, I couldn't disconnect from the somber thoughts weighing on me. The whole day had dragged. I was at my desk after everyone else had gone home for the evening. Sitting in the quiet, I kept looking over my phone feeling as if it was trying to get my attention. I was startled when it did vibrate its ring. The buzz seemed louder than normal. *Maybe it's Benny.* I had phoned him that day at about one p.m.; anxious to see how he was doing. When he didn't answer my call, it tapped on over to Voicemail. I left a short message for him to call me; hanging up with, "Love you, Benny."

I looked over at the screen and read "withheld number." *Shoot, it's not Benny.*

I pushed the talk button and cautiously said, "Hello?" A deep, serious male voice asked, "Is this Mr. Thomas Stewart?"

"Yes, it is," back to him.

A pause. "Uh, Mr. Stewart, this is the Black Diamond Police Department."

I was so used to getting calls from the police about the boys, I responded with, "Okay, which Stewart would it be this time?" I even added a slight chuckle.

I heard him clear his throat to say, "Mr. Stewart, I am calling about your son, Benjamin. Your son is Ben Stewart, correct?"

I nodded as if he could see me through the phone. The conversation was odd. I'd never heard such a flat tone in a voice like that before.

"Mr. Stewart, I am deeply sorry to inform you that your son is deceased."

I stopped breathing . . . I couldn't swallow . . . I couldn't move.

Before I let go my hold of the phone, I heard him say, ". . . drug overdose . . ."

The phone fell to the floor. I didn't want to pick it up. I didn't want to hear anymore.

I didn't need to hear what happened. I had prepared my heart long ago for the inevitable. I knew the odds stacked against two people so addicted to drugs were slim—but this dad losing a son to drugs was now one in two. Finally, I bent over to grab that stupid device that had only brought me bad news. I vaguely listened to where my son had been taken, then hung up before his good-bye. For twelve years, the phone had been my compass to tell me where I needed to go to rescue my boys. I'd jump up, hop in my car, as if I were wearing a *Dad, the Hero cape*, to go and save them.

Benny was dead. I couldn't save him this time. The lump in my throat and my tears came fast and heavy. I was numb. My head was burrowed in my arms soaked by tears. My eyes slammed shut to a surreal picture of Benny's face smiling so brightly—like the day he came to see me. The last day I would ever see him. The last hug I would ever get from *My Buddy*.

My intense crying brought out emotions I had never felt before. Not being able to move, I wondered if my body was in shock. Was it the undercurrent ache of resentment rising up in me for how a divorce sparked such brokenness in my children? That's when it all went wrong. I didn't want to blame, but that's all I had left.

I was picturing Benny's visit that day. "Thank you, Lord, that I was standing on that hill." I remembered how the words he said melted me. How he told me he didn't know what he would have done without me. *What am I going to do without him?* I sobbed.

My mind barricaded my pain. My boys sought out drugs to block theirs.

Still slumped over, the smile I could still see showed me that Benny was no longer a slave to the evil of drugs. Sadly, the recovery houses had not been enough and my house was not enough. The Lord's house is where he needed to be. My sorrow eased a little, knowing Benny was finally sober and safe at his forever home in heaven.

I did not go to the viewing. It was probably best that I didn't. My pastor was gracious enough to do that for me. I wanted to remember Benny's smiling face from the last day I saw him.

From the coroner's report, we learned the time of Benny's death was estimated at one p.m. He was found dead in the guest bedroom of his friend's home of an accidental overdose (pharmaceutical morphine and oxycodone intoxication).

The time of his death resonated with me. It was the same time I left my phone message for him. I sensed something strange that day when he didn't pick up his phone or call me back. I have a strong feeling that was not just a coincidence.

At his funeral, it was standing room only. It was evident what Benny's life had meant to others. All the dysfunctional particles of my life were awkwardly joined together that day to mourn my son.

Just below the microphone were the many flowers sent in memory of him. So many colors full of life. *Just like Benny.* On an easel on one side of the stage was a whimsical, hand-painted portrait, displaying my son's dynamic face. Then, the song began. The one my daughter Becca chose to sing. A most touching moment how she missed her brother. The immense chills cracked me open. Through the haze of my tears, I saw him come back to life for a while in a picture-by-picture video. My world as his daddy was revealed in one heartbreaking photo after another, fading in one day as my baby boy, fading out to his last picture taken by my side on what would be his last birthday.

When it was my turn to speak, whoever knew him already had some idea of what I would say. He was just that loved. He was unique.

I shared what it was like to be Benny's dad. How grateful I was for the twenty-three years I had with him. It was easier than talking about the years ahead I wouldn't have. Benny's heart had always been to help those trapped in addiction, even though he couldn't get free himself. I was now one of those grieving parents that I remembered the chaplain talking about. That sermon that haunted me from the day before he died, prepared me for the devastating news.

I also told a few quirky stories about him to console the tears falling around the room. My favorite was this, "When Benny was two, he was riding in the backseat while a very close friend of mine named Larry and I were riding in the front. Benny had always been overly protective of me—and that day was just hilarious. The entire three-hour car ride, Larry and I would try and talk. Benny would constantly interrupt Larry by repeating over and over again to him, "No . . . Larry . . . No!" As tickled as Larry was, he stepped out of the car, laughing, "I don't ever want to hear my name again!" Before I stepped down, I couldn't stress enough to the parents in that room to cherish the times with our children. A parent never knows if it will ever be them standing up there where I was.

Helium balloons were filled along with personal messages tucked inside. Written to Benny from all who loved him. Before they were released into the air, it was mine that still needed to be written. All what I wanted to say wouldn't fit on that little note of paper. Out of the novel I could have wrote, this is what I did write: "I love you, Benny, My Buddy." Watching my balloon float away, I took the phrase used at his funeral as my own and told him, "It's not good-bye, it's see you soon!"

Benny was twenty-three when he died. At the time, Brian was twenty-five. Since his brother's death, the countless attempts I've made for Brian have unraveled like a ball of yarn. Not even the death of his brother turned his life around.

Brian continued to walk out of several detox centers, rehabs, treatment centers, and at least six different recovery homes. I pray that someday his brother's death was not in vain in regards to Brian.

I constantly wait for him to reach out to me; always prepared to remind him, "When you are ready to go back to treatment, I will take you." *Lord, please guide my son to get well. I can't imagine losing another one.*

My life was rising from ashes; Benny's life ended in ashes. His body was cremated. What remained of his physical body is now in a black box, embellished with an eagle I consider as him. What remains of his heart, soul, mind, and spirit is in his last hug that wraps everything wonderful about him around me. It quenches a portion of my grief. A small part of Benny's ashes hang around my neck, with an eagle emblem dangling from the chain; he did earn Eagle Scout after all. Sadly, Brian did not. But, it was Benny who needed his wings for his legacy to take flight.

THIRTY-SIX

THE NUDGE

ON THE MORNING of December 31, 2015, I was in my den, pondering the last fifty-three years of my life, and the last thirty-five years since the abuse stopped. Swiveling in my black leather armchair to the pictures that hung on the wall, trying to cope with my heart that's bleeding inside. I don't know if these memories help me get through, or if they keep me shackled to my heartache? *I miss that boy! It's been a year and four and a half months; and, no . . . time has not made it any easier.*

My watch read 8:11 a.m. I had to do a double take. *Benny died on that day*—the eighth month on the eleventh day. I've got this thing—I know that God speaks to me through numbers. It never fails, any correlation of numbers that cross my path—whether it be on a clock, my cell phone, or a page I turn to in a book, the numbers relay a sign to me.

I paid close attention to what might come next. I waited. Then, it came to me. *The date was 12/31/2015. The numbers in 2015 add up to 8—the month Benny died. The 2 ones are for 11—the day he died. And, the remaining 2 and 3 signify his age of 23—when he died.* To me, it was a clear sign like no other. Like a message straight from God about Benny. It had to be. I closed my eyes hoping to see his face.

But it wasn't Benny's face that popped into my mind. Someone else's did. A face I didn't want to see.

Then, a revelation came to me as clear as the face I saw. It wasn't a message from God about Benny as much as it was a nudge. I knew exactly what it meant. Well, I guess this is what I am supposed to do with my day. I told my wife Rene' where I was headed. The look on her face confirmed why I needed to do this. With the printed directions in my hand, I headed out the door with her blessing.

The estimated travel time from point A to point B would be about fifty minutes. It was going to take me at least that long to formulate the words I needed to say. As for the courage part, I had a feeling that everything I had gone through in the past had conditioned me along the way. Maybe my hard times had been like workouts at a fitness club. I may have started out weak, but as each incident happened, strength and endurance grew. Anyway, that's the way I felt that day.

The entire way there, I tried to come up with what to say. Nothing came to mind. *What is there to say anyway?*

After exiting the freeway, I followed the directions with their twists and turns in the road. Up to this point, I had no reservations about my destination.

Then it got real. My heart started to beat faster. Soon it was pounding my chest. I pulled over and parked on the side of the road and asked myself, *Are you emotionally up for this?* Taking a sip of water out of my water bottle, I felt my stomach want to throw it right back up again. Adrenaline was intensifying in my body.

Why am I doing this? I didn't take long to answer myself, *Because, dummy, God told you to.*

Gathering up my confidence, I pulled back out on the road. After driving down some side streets, I came to the last stop sign before the turn I was supposed to take.

Pretending Benny was sitting in my passenger seat as my navigator helped. I knew I couldn't let him down, so I kept going. After I took the right-hand turn, I said out loud, "This is it. This is the road," as if Benny really were sitting next to me. With my car creeping down the street at almost an idle, I scanned house by house for the right number. I froze as I found it there on the left.

I parked down the street out of the line of sight where the house was still visible from my side mirror. *You didn't come all this way to hide out,* I told myself as I opened the door and stepped out; determined to see this through. Both of my hands reached up to wrap around the part of Benny I carried around my neck. As I walked, I felt stronger and less nervous with each step. *Thank you, My Buddy.*

I was caught off guard by a man who came out of the house I was walking toward. On the sidewalk, I casually asked him if he knew the person I was there to see.

"I'm his brother-in-law," he said. Then he led me right up to the front door.

Partially cracking open the door, he called out, "Hey, there is someone here to see you."

My pulse started racing as I heard footsteps from inside the house coming toward me. I'm surprised my heart didn't stop, because it felt like my breathing had. There he was . . . standing in the doorway right in front of me. Bruce himself. The look on his face was the same incredulous look that my wife had when I told her where I was going that day.

His brother-in-law started to introduce me, saying, "This is . . ." Bruce cleared his throat and interrupted with a dry, "Yeah, I know who he is." He didn't extend his hand to shake mine.

All I could think was, *This is a huge mistake.* His expression was not welcoming. I didn't know why I expected anything else.

Bruce opened the door the rest of the way to make his way outside as his brother-in-law excused himself.

Thirty-five years had gone by since the last time he and I had been alone together. I struggled to get ahold of myself and keep my head straight.

We talked about nothing much. His manner was withdrawn and his voice low. His demeanor was as if nothing bad had ever happened between us. I couldn't tell if there was any remorse in his subdued mannerisms. *Not my problem. I'll leave that one alone.* I wasn't there to chat or shoot the breeze anyway.

I remembered his claim from way back of finding God. I just hoped and prayed that was still true. I didn't wait long for a break to say what I needed to. "Bruce, I am here because I want to tell you face-to-face that I forgive you for what happened."

Silence.

His reaction was not what I expected. I wasn't sure what I had expected. I just knew that the hostile look on his face was my invitation to leave. I didn't expect him to shake hands good-bye, and he didn't. But it was the words he shot out that shook me. "I hope this means you and Matt are done lying about all of this." He turned and walked away.

I was shaking some as I got into my car, but as I started to drive home, I felt calmer.

The fear in my head was gone. I had just survived a crash course in forgiveness—the reason I had gone there in the first place.

For thirty-five years, I needed help to forgive Bruce. *How was I supposed to forgive a man like that?*

I knew I had a choice to either continue to bury the pain, or finally get rid of it. Burying the pain hadn't worked for me. It was clear God knew better and had gently nudged me to do something about it. It took me until I pulled into my driveway to fully grasp how I felt. I wasn't expecting some miraculous apology from Bruce—I learned that from way back when my mother didn't believe me . . . but, that's not what my visit was for.

I sat in my car for a while, thanking God for the peace He had just given to me. In awe, I thought, *I will take this form of His blessings any day!*

I DO matter! I know that now. It took me this long to realize that I never needed my mom to believe me to make it so . . .

EPILOGUE

NO MATTER WHAT

I NEVER IMAGINED my own life story was going to be published with its dramatic themes of horrific abuse, chaos, loss, and tragedy. The little bit of humor in the mix is what kept me sane. Thanking Jesus for that. The Lord has delivered me from the emotional damage of those afflictions, and has redeemed them by equipping me to help free other victims who are still held captive by the chains of their past; using it for His good.

The original title for this book was going to be 'No Matter What', meaning a faith in Jesus Christ will carry you through whatever trials you are faced with in this life and bring you to healing—no matter what.

I've accepted the life I was dealt. That acceptance has helped minimize the effects of Bruce's abuse that might have otherwise have ruined me. Maybe all the distractions enabled me to move past the damage. Maybe they kept me afloat, rather than sinking into the abyss, as so many other victims do.

My upbringing was a breeding ground well-suited for a pedophile. With Bruce living just a few houses away, he had scoped out my brother and me. Just as statistics warn, he became familiar with our family dynamics and groomed us. He knew just how much to insert himself into our family to fill the void left by my workaholic dad. Mom was into perfectionism—whatever would help us achieve. Bruce convinced her he was just the one to get us to Eagle Scout.

When the abuse began, I was too young to catch on. Even if I had, saying no to any authority was forbidden. I was just an excited kid who wanted to earn as many skill awards and merit badges as he could get. Bruce promised me I would get what I wanted with his help—as long as he got what he wanted in the process.

Being a "teacher's pet" gave me some self-worth after my mother's constant criticism. I wanted nothing more than to be Bruce's Prize Scout. He made me feel special and a chosen one—for a while anyway—until he wormed his way into my psyche.

Playing doctor was kind of a secret "no-no" normal to an eight-year-old boy—especially when my mother scared the natural, little boy curiosity right out of me. To get away from the grip of her control, I rose to the challenge and defied her.

Bruce's mental games escalated until they were way over my head. I didn't know better. Once I did, his manipulative mind control took over. My voice—my "No"—was silenced by the threat of a gun that did the talking for him. The fear from his threats to kill my family tied my hands and gagged my mouth.

"How did it go on so long?" you might wonder. Until eighteen? Really? When a child is unfortunately brainwashed, abused, and threatened from a young age, fear paralyzes and subverts reality.

The day my mom didn't believe me was the final blow to my self-worth. But that changed the day my brother Matt's revelations opened the gates of what happened to us in our childhoods. He led the way to unwrap what was hidden underneath my denial. When the attorney took our case, it was pivotal, as he believed us when our own mother did not.

Not coming to terms with my abuse until I was forty years old built up entrenched coping mechanisms that have taken time to subside. I hung on to my Stewart family pride like it was normal and used sarcasm to hide what was simmering in my soul. With the Holy Spirit and my wife's positive, but firm, support, I am learning to replace those traits with much-needed tact, and to be confident, not arrogant. My, "lay low and be quiet" passivity has been transforming as my self-esteem grows.

The nightmares are still as real as they have always been. They come at random, and sometimes attack more powerfully than ever. For the most part, my brain still resides in lockdown. I think my mind allows just what I can handle to surface. I take that as a gift to protect my heart. I don't feel there is a need to bring up those things that God has already taken away.

Prayer has kept me sane, peace comforts me, and the blessings to come are what keep me going. In understanding the reasons for the abuse, chaos, and loss in my life, one scripture greatly helps me: "You intended to harm me, but God intended it for good to accomplish what is now being done, the saving of many lives" (Genesis 50:20). I hold it near and dear to my heart.

Bruce intended to harm me, but God has used my voice to raise awareness on the lax accountability of the Scouts and other youth organizations that are the potential hunting grounds of pedophiles. Our landmark court case aided in the 2012 ruling that released a portion of the "perversion files" to the American public and shed light on how widespread the problem had been, bringing accountability to the Boy Scouts. Hopefully, many vulnerable young lives will be protected from abuse.

The cancer I contracted from hazardous workplace carcinogens intended to harm me. God's goodness cured me for a purpose—my work that includes responsibility for eliminating carcinogens in the workplace. Thirty years later, I was transferred to a different location to do the same—to save many more lives from unnecessary toxic exposure.

Divorce in my life has been very harmful, especially to my children. It drove my sons to addiction, tragically leading to my son's fatal overdose. How can I see God's goodness in my son's death? Benny is no longer suffering. I have been moved to tears by those who have specifically sought me out to tell me my son's death was not wasted. At least two of Benny's friends stopped using drugs altogether because of him. It is meaningful to me if his death saves even one life; I thank God for the hope of saving many more lives.

Without my faith in God, I honestly doubt I would be here today. I lean on the words of Isaiah 40:29-31:

> He gives strength to the weary and increases the power of the weak. Even youths grow tired and weary, and young men stumble and fall; but those who hope in the LORD will renew their strength. They will soar on wings like eagles; they will run and not grow weary, they will walk and not be faint.

I embrace the compassion that my difficult circumstances have given me. Seemingly, it takes the sacrifice of suffering for compassion and understanding to grow. I've learned how to understand the weary, the weak, and the faint—because I was one of them.

Throughout my trials, God has helped me in my weakness, increased my endurance and has created strength and resilience in me. God's help has left me no other choice than to submit my will. That is not weakness—it's pure courage! Nothing is more powerful than that.

My purpose in life is be an advocate for how faith in God can sustain us. I want to help those who are too broken to rise up on their own, to encourage them to overcome—and ultimately be able to help others themselves.

I say to children of a verbally abusive parent, sexual abuse victims, those who are suffering with—or have suffered with—cancer, parents of drug-addicted children, those having endured divorce, or have lost a child—I hear you, I can relate.

God's grace and mercy sustained me in everything I went through. I want to share that grace and mercy. I know what it is to wallow in my pain when it was consuming me deep from the inside, and want to help others who have suffered and are suffering. I want to encourage those experiencing abuse not to allow the bitterness and the evil that it came from to consume them, but to strive to understand the why, and overcome as victors instead of victims.

Finally, I've learned that forgiveness is what releases us and sets us free on the path to healing and freedom. You do your part, and God will do His. If you are unable or don't know how, pray, and ask God to show you how. When your response to the wrong done to you is fueled by forgiveness, you will see a miracle set in motion.

My pivotal moment came through a lesson from the life of a good friend of mine, Dean Smith of Live to Forgive Ministries. He forgave his stepfather, Bob, for taking the life of his mother. I had read what the Bible says about forgiveness, but Dean's words resonated in me. I knew if someone could forgive another person for doing something so horrific, I needed to listen.

Dean says, "Forgiveness is the gateway to experiencing the best life God has for me. Through His love, my focus was redirected from my tragedy to His awesome grace. Get honest with God about the 'Bobs' in your life."

My "Bob" was Bruce.

Dean also said, "One step of forgiveness can lead to a lifetime of blessings."

The day I extended forgiveness to Bruce, I walked away with some of those blessings he spoke of; starting with my heart . . . it broke free . . . and began heading down the pathway to healing.

Unfortunately, my own father, Robert "Bob" Stewart, just happens to be the latest "Bob" that popped open in my life.

My breakthrough with Bruce on that last day of 2015 confirmed the idea of this book. God said "go." With that in mind, I approached my dad and got his take. When I mentioned to him what the book was about, he was standoffish. My dad initially had become aware of what happened to my brother and me the same time of the court proceedings when I was 40. We never discussed it in detail, as I assumed he might be ashamed since my childhood was supposed to be on his watch.

From way-back-when, to then, and now, his Stewart pride is still as vivid as it always has been. Thirty-six years after my mother didn't believe me . . . It is still unclear whether my dad does or not.

No matter what, if your child comes to you and tells you something of this nature, please . . . please . . . listen!

I pray that the warning signs mentioned in this book will bring awareness to hopefully prevent sexual abuse from happening to another child.

ACKNOWLEDGMENTS

I'M OVERWHELMED WITH the blessings that brought me through to the good, after passing through the bad and the ugly. Without these trials in my life, I wouldn't be fit to help others who have gone through the same. Without the Lord, I wouldn't be here at all. I am full of utter thankfulness to be able to share my heart through this book.

God gave my wife Rene', "the one my heart loves" (Song 3:4), the gift of delving into my heart so she could write down my memories in this book, as if she could see into my mind.

I am thankful for my family who stuck with me—Rene's family, her children; significant others included, my church family, and my friends—for your love and support throughout. I pray the ones estranged from me will someday heal from their wounds, and my prodigal son will be freed. I love you—no matter what.

I am so grateful for the ones who contributed to this most personal venture through funds, encouragement, and prayer. Thank you for believing in us and having faith in my story.

Redemption is happening all over the place through the vision of a pastor and his wife. Thank you so much, Pastor Ross Holtz aka Dr. Ross Holtz, for all your support over the years, and for sharing breakfast with me that morning, sparking the idea of writing a book in the first place. And with who better? The one whom your own heart loves. Thank you,

Athena Dean Holtz and Redemption Press, for embracing my story and going with it.

Thank you to our editor, Inger Logelin, for your knowledge, wisdom, and patience in the whirlwind of information given to you to make it the best it could be. Besides squeezing out all the excessive adjectives I loved to overuse.

As for my other pastor, Marcus Kelly, thank you for friendship and support, especially taking on and facing the hard stuff with the death of my son. I appreciate your moral support through my toughest moments, and thereafter.

Thank you, Zane Thompson, for being the friend I never really had before. You are the mastermind behind the title and an integral part of my life. We have shared some very emotional, as well as hysterical moments I will never forget. We appreciate all you do. Love you, brother.

Thanks, Portillo family, for your love, friendship and humor that enhanced our lives through two puppies.

Thanks to you, Dean Smith of Live to Forgive Ministries. You have given me confidence like no other. Thank you for your humor and your wisdom to help me, and so many others.

Finally, my heartfelt appreciation goes to my brother, Matt. Without him, I would still be stuck in the shoving-it-down-deep mode. His boldness enabled me to arrive at knowing what it really means to forgive.

CONTACT INFORMATION

REDEMPTION
PRESS

To order additional copies of this book, please visit
www.redemption-press.com.
Also available on Amazon.com and BarnesandNoble.com
Or by calling toll free 1-844-2REDEEM.